So, you v Boul

By Stu Armstrong & Ryder Scott

ISBN: 9798589982763

Copyright © 2014 Stu Armstrong

All rights reserved.

1st Edition.

www.stuarmstrong.com

No part of this book may be copied or reproduced in any way shape or form without the express permission of the Author.

©Stu Armstrong 2014.

Contents

ACKNOWLEDGEMENTS 2

FOREWORD 5

RYDER'S BOOK DEDICATION 7

STU ARMSTRONG ON RYDER SCOTT 9

WAYNE SOUTHBY ON RYDER SCOTT 11

CHAPTER ONE 12

    THE HISTORY..12

CHAPTER TWO 18

    SOCIOLOGY..18

CHAPTER 3 24

    REGULATION AND TRAINING..24

CHAPTER FOUR 28

    FAMOUS BOUNCERS...28

CHAPTER FIVE 31

    OLD SCHOOL VS NEW SCHOOL 31

CHAPTER SIX 43

    WHAT'S IT REALLY LIKE?..43

CHAPTER SEVEN 60

    A MODERN DAY BOUNCERS ROLE 60

CHAPTER EIGHT 66

    WHAT MAKES A GOOD BOUNCER 66

CHAPTER NINE 70

    THE SIA 70

CHAPTER TEN 74

    HOW DO I BECOME A BOUNCER 74

CHAPTER ELEVEN 84

    TRAINING 84

CHAPTER TWELVE **93**

LEARNING MODUALES 93
Module 1: Working in the Private Security Industry *93*
Module 2: Working as a Door Supervisor *97*
Module 3: Conflict Management *101*
Module 4: Physical Intervention Skills for the Private Security Industry *103*

CHAPTER THIRTEEN **109**

CHOOSING THE RIGHT TRAINING 109

CHAPTER 14 ...... **114**

TESTS 114

CHAPTER FIFETEEN **120**

UPSKILLING 120

CHAPTER SIXTEEN **123**

APPLYING INFO FOR SIA LICENCE 123

CHAPTER FIFTEEN - SA **128**

LOOKING FOR A JOB 128

CHAPTER SEVENTEEN **131**

HOW TO DEAL WITH THE AFTER EFFECTS OF VIOLENCE FOR THE FIRST TIME 131

CHAPTER EIGHTEEN - COMPLETE **149**

DO'S AND DON'TS 149
ABOUT THE AUTHORS 152
STU ARMSTRONG 152
RYDER SCOTT 154

Chapter One

The History

The history of 'Bouncers' or 'Doorman' can be seen going back into ancient history, the significance of the doorman as the person allowing or barring entry is found in a number of Greek myths with such quotes as "Overcoming the seven doormen guarding the gates to the Underworld". Also in the old testament of the bible, specifically in Chronicles 26 of the Old Testament, with the 'Levitical Temple' described as having a number of 'Gatekeepers' who were there to protect the temple from theft and from illegal entries into sacred areas, all of these tasks are shared with the modern concept of the bouncer.

The Romans had a position known as the 'Ostiarius' which translates to 'Doorkeeper', initially a slave, who guarded the door, and ejected unwanted's from the house he guarded. The term later become a low-ranking clergy title Plautus, in his play Bacchides (written approximately 194–184 BC), mentions a "large and powerful" man as a threat to get an unwelcome visitor to leave.

Tertullian, an early Christian author living mainly in the 1st century AD, while reporting on the casual oppression of Christians in Carthage, noted that bouncers were counted as part of a semi-legal underworld, amongst other 'shady' characters such as gamblers and pimps.

During the late 19th and early 20th centuries, US saloon-keepers and brothel madams hired bouncers to remove troublesome, violent, or drunk patrons, and protect the saloon girls and prostitutes.

The word "bouncer" was first popularized in a novel by Horatio Alger, Jr., called The Young Outlaw, published in 1875. Alger was an immensely popular author in the 19th century. In a chapter called "Bounced", a boy is thrown out of a restaurant because he has no money to pay for his dinner:

"Here, Peter, you waited on this young man, didn't you?" "Yes, sir." "He hasn't paid for his breakfast, and pretends he hasn't got any money. Bounce him!" If Sam was ignorant of the meaning of the word 'bounce,' he was soon enlightened. The waiter seized him by the collar, before he knew what was going to happen, pushed him to the door, and then, lifting his foot by a well-directed kick, landed him across the sidewalk into the street. This proceeding was followed by derisive laughter from the other waiters who had gathered near the door, and it was echoed by two street urchins outside, who witnessed Sam's ignominious exit from the restaurant. Sam staggered from the force of the bouncing, and felt disgraced and humiliated to think that the waiter who had been so respectful and attentive should have inflicted upon him such an indignity, which he had no power to resent.

An 1883 newspaper article stated that "'The Bouncer' is merely the English 'chucker out'. When liberty verges on license and gaiety on wanton delirium, the Bouncer selects the gayest of the gay, and — bounces him!

In an Arizona saloon in 1885, from the era when bouncers earned their rough and tumble reputation by forcibly ejecting brawlers.

In US Western towns in the 1870s, high-class brothels hired bouncers for security and to prevent patrons from evading payment. For security, somewhere in every parlor house there was always a bouncer, a man who stayed sober to handle any customer who got too rough with one of the girls or didn't want to pay.

The presence of bouncers in high-class brothels was one of the reasons the girls considered themselves superior to lower-class free-lancers, who lacked any such protection.

In the late 19th century, until Prohibition, bouncers also had the unusual role of protecting the saloon's buffet. To attract business, many saloons lured customers with offers of a free lunch, which was usually well salted to inspire drinking, and the saloon Bouncer was generally on hand to discourage those with hearty appetites.

In the late 19th century, bouncers at small town dances and bars physically resolved disputes and removed troublemakers, without worrying about lawsuits. It has been said that there were many quarrels and many fights, but all were settled on the spot. There were no court costs, only some aches and pains for the troublemakers.

In the 1880s and 1890s, bouncers were used to maintain order in the "The Gut", the roughest part of New **York's** Coney Island, which was filled with ramshackle groups of wooden shanties, bars, cabarets, fleabag hotels and brothels. Huge bouncers patrolled these venues of vice and roughly ejected anyone who violated the loose rules of decorum by engaging in pick-pocketing, or fights.

During the 1890s, San Diego had a similarly rough waterfront area and red-light district called the Stingaree, where bouncers worked the door at brothels. Prostitutes worked at the area's 100 or so brothels in small rooms, paying a fee to the protector who usually was the bouncer of the brothel.

The more expensive, higher-class brothels were called parlor houses, to maintain the high-class atmosphere at these establishments, male patrons were expected to act like gentlemen, and if any customer did or said anything out of line, he was asked to leave. A bouncer made sure he did.

Bouncers in pre-World War I United States were also sometimes used as the guardians of morality. As ballroom dancing was often considered as an activity which could lead to immoral conduct if the dancers got too close, some of the more reputable venues had bouncers to remind patrons not to dance closer than nine inches to their partners. The bouncer's warnings tended to consist of light taps on the shoulder at first, and then progressed to more decisive actions.

In the 1930s, bars in the roughest parts of Baltimore docks hired bouncers to maintain order and eject aggressive customers. It is reputed that the Oasis club, operated by Max Cohen, hired a lady bouncer by the name of Mickey Steele, a six-foot acrobat from the Pennsylvania coal fields. Mickey was always considerate of the people she bounced, first asking them where they lived and then throwing them in that general direction! She was succeeded by a character known as 'Machine-Gun Butch' who was a long-time bouncer at the club".

In the Weimar Republic in Germany of the 1920s and early 1930s, doormen protected venues from the fights caused by Nazis and other potentially violent groups like the Communists. Such scenes can be seen in the movie Cabaret. Hitler surrounded himself with a number of former bouncers such as Christian Weber, the **SS** originated as a group designated to protect party meetings and was made up from Bouncers. In early Nazi Germany, some bouncers in underground jazz clubs were also hired to screen for Nazi spies, because jazz was considered a degenerate form of music by the Nazi party.

Later during the Nazi regime, bouncers also increasingly barred non-German people from public functions, such as dances at dance halls. Bouncers also often come into conflict with football hooligans, due to the tendency of groups of hooligans to congregate at pubs and bars before and after games. In the United Kingdom for example, a long-running series of feuds between groups of hooligans and groups of bouncers were well documented in the 1990s.

Bouncers have also been known to be associated with criminal gangs, especially in places like Russia, Hong Kong or Japan, where bouncers may often belong to these groups or have to pay the crime syndicates to be able to operate. In Hong Kong, Triad connected reprisal or intimidation attacks against bouncers are a common occurrence.

Hong Kong also features a somewhat unusual situation where some bouncers are known to work for prostitutes, instead of being their pimps. Hong Kong police have noted that they sometimes had to charge the bouncer for illegally extorting money from the women, when the usually expected dominance situation between the sex worker and her 'protector' was in fact reversed.

Bouncing has also started to attract some academic interest as part of studies into violent subcultures. Bouncers were selected as one of the groups studied by several English researchers in the 1990s because their culture was seen as 'grounded in violence', as well as because the group had increasingly been 'demonised' by the general public.

Chapter Two

Sociology

In the early 1990s, an Australian government study on violence stated that violent incidents in public drinking venues are caused by the interaction of five factors:

1. Aggressive and unreasonable bouncers.
2. Groups of male strangers.
3. Low comfort (e.g., unventilated, hot clubs)
4. High boredom
5. Drunkenness

The research indicated that bouncers did not play as large a role as expected in the creation of an aggressive or violent atmosphere, however, the study did show that edgy and aggressive bouncers, especially when they are petty in their manner, do have an adverse effect.

The study stated that bouncers:

"Have been observed to initiate fights or further encourage them on several occasions. Many seem poorly trained, obsessed with their own machismo, and relate badly to groups of male strangers. Some of them appear to regard their employment as giving them a license to assault people. This may be encouraged by management adherence to a repressive model of supervision of patrons, which in fact does not reduce trouble, and exacerbates an already hostile and aggressive situation. In practice many bouncers are not well managed in their work, and appear to be given a job autonomy and discretion that they cannot handle well"

One major study also observed bouncing from within, as part of a British project to study violent subcultures. Beyond studying the bouncer culture from the outside, the group selected a suitable candidate for covert, long-term research. The man had previously worked as a bouncer before becoming an academic. The study has, however, attracted some criticism due to the fact that the researcher, while fulfilling his duties as a bouncer and being required to set aside his academic distance, would have been at risk of losing objectivity.

One of the main ethical issues of the research was the participation of the researcher in violence, and to what degree he would be allowed to participate. The group could not fully resolve this issue, as the undercover researcher would not have been able to gain the trust of his peers while shying away from the use of force. As part of the study it eventually became clear that bouncers themselves were similarly and constantly weighing up the limits and uses of their participation in violence. The research however found that instead of being a part of the occupation, violence itself was the defining characteristic, a "culture created around violence and violent expectation"

The bouncing culture's insular attitudes also extended to the recruitment process, which was mainly by word of mouth as opposed to typical job recruitment, and also depended heavily on previous familiarity with violence. This does not extend to the prospective bouncer himself having to have a reputation for violence, rather a perception was needed that he could deal with it if required. Various other elements, such as body language or physical looks (muscles, shaved heads) were also described as often expected for entry into bouncing being part of the symbolic 'narratives of intimidation' that set bouncers apart in their work environment.

Training on the job was described as very limited, with the new bouncers being 'thrown into the deep end', the fact that they had been accepted for the job in the first place including the assessment that they should know what they are doing.

In the case of the British research project, the legally required licensing as a bouncer was also found to be expected by employers before applicants started the job, and as licensing generally excluded people with criminal convictions, this kept out some of the more unstable violent personalities.

I am not sure just how much of that I actually believe or is actually true but the study does raise some interesting points, which if applied in this day and age I don't think you would find commonplace, I believe that much of this study is based around what are termed as 'Old School Bouncers'.

Whilst some of the 'Old School' values and methods are very much missed these days, I am a believer that the best bouncers don't "Bounce" anyone unless there is no other option…………………………………….... they talk to people.

An ability to judge and communicate well with people will reduce the need for physical intervention, while a steady personality will prevent the bouncer from being easily provoked by customers. Bouncers also profit from good written communication skills, because they are often required to document assaults in an incident log or using an incident form. Well-kept incident logs can protect the employee from any potential criminal charges which can often later arise from an incident.

However, British research from the 1990s also indicates that a major part of both the group identity and the job satisfaction of bouncers is related to their self-image as a strongly masculine person who is capable of dealing with, and dealing out, violence. Their employment income plays a lesser role in their job satisfaction. Bouncer subculture is strongly influenced by perceptions of honor and shame, a typical characteristic of groups that are constantly in the public eye.

Factors in enjoying work as a bouncer were also found in the general prestige and respect that was accorded to bouncers, sometimes bordering on hero worship. The camaraderie between bouncers, was also often cited.

The same research has also indicated that the decisions made by bouncers, while seeming haphazard to an outsider, often have a basis in rational logic. The decision to turn certain customers away at the door because of too casual clothing is for example often based on the perception that the person will be more willing to fight compared to someone dressed in expensive attire. Many similar decisions taken by a bouncer during the course of a night are also being described as based on experience rather than just personality.

Movies often depict bouncers physically throwing patrons out of clubs and restraining drunk customers with headlocks, which has led to a popular misconception that bouncers have or reserve the right to use physical force freely. However, in many countries bouncers have no legal authority to use physical force more freely than any other civilian, meaning they are restricted to reasonable levels of force used in self-defense, to eject drunk or aggressive patrons refusing to leave a venue, or when restraining a patron who has committed an offence until police arrive

According to statistical research in Canada, bouncers are as likely to face physical violence in their work as urban-area police officers. The research also found that the likelihood of such encounters increased with the number of years the bouncer their worked in his occupation. Despite popular misconceptions, bouncers in Western countries are normally unarmed. Some bouncers may carry weapons such as expandable batons for personal protection, but they may not have a legal right to carry a weapon even if they would prefer to do so.

Use of force training programs teach bouncers ways to avoid using force and explain what types of force are considered allowable by the courts. Some bars have gone so far as to institute policies barring physical contact, where bouncers are instructed to ask a drunk or disorderly patron to leave, if the patron refuses, the bouncers call police. However, if the police are called too frequently, it can reflect badly on the venue upon renewal of its license.

Another strategy used in some bars is to hire smaller, less threatening or female bouncers, because they may be better able to defuse conflicts than large, intimidating bouncers which are also often challenged by aggressive males wanting to prove their machismo.

Large and intimidating bouncers, whilst providing an appearance of strong security, may also drive customers away in cases where a more relaxed environment is desired. In addition, female security staff, apart from having fewer problems searching female patrons for drugs or weapons and entering women's toilets to check for illegal activities, are also considered as better able to deal with drunk or aggressive women.

In Australia, for example, women comprise almost 20% of the security industry and increasingly work the door as well, using "a smile, chat and a friendly but firm demeanor" to resolve tense situations. Nearly one in nine of Britain's nightclub bouncers are also women, with the UK's 2003 Licensing Act giving the authorities "discretionary power to withhold a venue's license if it does not employ female door staff. This is credited with having opened the door for women to enter the profession. However, female bouncers are still a rarity in many countries, such as in India, where two women who became media celebrities in 2008 for being **Punjab**'s first female bouncers but were soon sacked again after accusations of unbecoming behavior.

Chapter 3

Regulation and training

In many countries, a bouncer must be licensed and lacking a criminal record to gain employment within the security sector. In some countries or regions, bouncers may be required to have extra skills or special licenses and certification for first aid, alcohol distribution, crowd control, or fire safety.

In Canada, bouncers have the right to use reasonable force to expel intoxicated or aggressive patrons. First, the patron must be asked to leave the premises. If the patron refuses to leave, the bouncer can use reasonable force to expel the patron. This has been upheld in a number of court cases. Under the definition of 'reasonable force', "it is perfectly acceptable for the bouncer to grab a patron's arm to remove the patron from the premises. However, only in situations where employees reasonably believe that the conduct of the patron puts them in danger can they inflict harm on a patron and then only to the extent that such force is necessary for self-defense.

In British Columbia, door staff are required to become certified under the Ministry of Public Safety and Solicitor General Office. The course called Basic Security Training, is a 40 hour program that covers law, customer service, and other issues related to security operation.

In Alberta USA, all bar and nightclub security staff had to take a, government-run training course on correct bouncer behavior and skills before the end of 2008. The six-hour

'ProTect' course will, among other subjects, teach staff to identify conflicts before they become violent, and how to defuse situations without resorting to force.[

In Ontario, courts have ruled that a tavern owes a twofold duty of care to its patrons. It must ensure that it does not serve alcohol which would apparently intoxicate or increase the patron's intoxication. As well, it must take positive steps to protect patrons and others from the dangers of intoxication.

Regarding the second requirement of protecting patrons, the law holds that customers cannot be ejected from your premises if doing so would put them in danger for example, due to the patron's intoxication. Bars can be held liable for ejecting a customer who they know, or should know, is at risk of injury by being ejected. Also in Ontario, bartenders and servers have to have completed the 'Smart Serve' Training Program, which teaches them to recognise the signs of intoxication. The Smart Serve program is also recommended for other staff in bars who have contact with potentially intoxicated patrons, such as bouncers. This certification program encourages bars to keep incident logs, to use as evidence if an incident gets to court. Since August 2007 with the advent of the Private Security and Investigative Services Act, Ontario law also requires security industry workers, including bouncers to be licensed.

In New Zealand, since 2011, Bouncers have been required to have a Certificate of approval. Like other security work, the person who has the COA has been vetted by the Police and cleared through security checks, as well as the Courts to show the person is suitable for the job, and knows New Zealand law to prevent going to Court for using excessive force and assault on Patrons

Singapore requires all bouncers to undergo a background check and attend a five day National Skills Recognition System course for security staff. However, many of the more professional security companies and larger venues with their own dedicated security staff have noted that the course is insufficient for the specific requirements of a bouncer and provide their own additional training.

Here in the UK, 'Door Supervisors' or 'Stewards' in Scotland as they are termed, must hold a license from the Security Industry Authority. The training for a door supervisor license includes issues such as behavior, conflict management, civil and criminal law, search and arrest procedures, drug awareness, recording of incidents and crime scene preservation, licensing law, equal opportunities and discrimination, health and safety at work, physical intervention, and emergency procedures. Licenses must be renewed every three years. Licensed door supervisors must wear license, which is often worn on the upper arm, whilst on duty.

The 2010 UK quango reforms includes the SIA amongst many other Quangos the coalition government intended it to be disbanded, on the overall grounds of cost, despite the SIA being essentially self-funding via license payments. Whilst this may alleviate to some extent the financial burden on employers and individuals alike, some members of the industry sees this as a retrograde step, fearing a return of the organized criminal element to the currently regulated industry.

In the Republic of Ireland all potential Bouncers must complete a FETAC Level Four course in Door Security Procedures. This allows them to apply for a Private Security

Authority license. The PSA vet all applicants before issuing a license, some past convictions will disqualify an applicant from working in the security industry. The license issued by the PSA entitles the holder of the license to work in pubs, clubs and event security.

In the USA requirements for bouncers vary from state to state, with some examples being, for example in California, Senate

Bill 194 requires any bouncer or security guard to be registered with the State of California Department of Consumer Affairs Bureau of Security and Investigative Services. These guards must also complete a criminal background check, including submitting their fingerprints to the California Department of Justice and the Federal Bureau of Investigation. Californians must undertake the Skills Training Course for Security Guards before receiving a security license. Further courses allow for qualified security personnel to carry batons upon completion of training.

In New York State, it is illegal for a bar owner to knowingly hire a felon for a bouncer position. Under Article 7 General Business Law, bars and nightclubs are not allowed to hire bouncers without a proper license. Under New York state law only a Private Investigator, Guard and Patrol Agency can supply Bouncers to bars.

Chapter Four

Famous Bouncers

In all walks of life and all professions you get people that move on to bigger and better things as it were, those that head down a different career path from the one in which they started and end up famous for whatever reason, it's just the same for Doorman, Here are just a few famous people that at one point in their lives worked the door. Some of the names won't exactly come as a shock to you, but some of them will.

A somewhat unusual example is Jorge Mario Bergoglio, the current Pope who worked as a bouncer in a Buenos Aires bar to earn money as a student. Dave Batista, former WWE superstar, worked as a bouncer in Washington D.C. nightclubs prior to his wrestling career and Al Capone, Chicago-based gangster, worked as a Bouncer in his early life.

Geoff Thompson, British bouncer and author of the book Watch My Back which was turned into the movie 'Clubbed' worked the doors for many years and Glenn Ross, Northern Irish and strongman still does.

James Gandolfini, American actor best known a Tony Soprano worked as a bouncer at an on-campus pub while studying at Rutgers University and Michael Clarke Duncan, American actor not only worked as a Bouncer but also as a bodyguard for various celebrities.

The legend that is Lenny McLean, British bare-knuckle boxing heavyweight champion was a well-documented Bouncer who worked as a head doorman in many London nightclubs.

Mr. T, American actor, is not only a former bouncer but also was twice winner of the "America's Toughest Bouncer" competition. Another hard man that was a Bouncer at one time is Bas Rutten, the Dutch Mixed Martial Artist and kickboxer as was Chris Kesterson, the Bare-knuckle.

Vin Diesel, American actor who created his 'Vin Diesel' pseudonym to protect his anonymity while working as a bouncer actually created a TV series based around his experiences on the doors named 'The Ropes', also Swedish actor and director Dolph Lundgrenn is known to have also been in the game.

Ironically the star of the movie 'Roadhouse' Patrick Swayze, was once a Bouncer, reputedly the movie was based on Ivan 'Doc' Holiday, Canadian bouncer and author of The Cooler's Grimiore and who has starred in a number of reality TV shows, ands who is very knowledgable in the trade and a staunch opponent to the SIA in the UK.

Norman Foster, British Architect and member of the House of Lords, worked as a night club bouncer whilst studying architecture at the University of Manchester, and not to forget the two authors of this very book, Ryder Scott, star of Channel 4's documentary series 'Bouncers' and Stu Armstrong author of 'The Diaries of a Doorman' series of books.

Chapter Five

Old School vs New School

Question... how can you spot an old school doorman? Answer... when the lights come on at the end of the night they do not attempt to clear the venue cos they are too busy scouring the floor for money!

Seriously though, when I was researching for this book, I thought I best find out where 'old school' originated from and for what purpose the saying was developed. I thought it was a fairly new saying as I first heard it to describe older styles of music, which caused me to dislike the saying when people referred to me as an 'old school doorman' because I just never put the two together. However when I did a bit of internet digging I found that the saying old school originates from 1749 as an adjective and simply notes that it's a compound of the words old and school, in reference to conservative beliefs or principles.

This confirms that it's related to an "old school of thought", however the modern slang sense of old school is somewhat different, with stronger connotations of respect for an earlier era. It is also referred to anything that may be considered old-fashioned. The term is commonly used to suggest a high regard for something that has been shown to have lasting value or quality. So when I look at it again if people want to call me old school then it either says they have a respect for me being from an earlier era or I am old-fashioned and have some lasting values with quality.

But of course this does not solely relate to me, as it can include almost every long serving door supervisor whether they are still actively working or not, it can also be referenced to fairly new door supervisors who have 'old school' tendencies. For example after my appearance on Channel 4's Bouncers I was befriended on Facebook and Twitter by hundreds of people and I have kept in contact with many of them and I try my best to reply to the many messages I get asking for advice. One such doorman – Dom – complimented me on my philosophy and referred to me as 'old school' like himself, so there is the proof that if you look at the definition *"a high regard for something that has been shown to have lasting value or quality"* then I fall into that category as someone else has complimented me on my regard for the values and quality I displayed.

Dom himself has been working the doors of London for as long, if not longer than I have so to be compliment by a fellow old school doorman was a relief as I was shitting myself before the series was aired. Likewise when many other old school doormen contacted me and complimented me, including Stu, hence the birth of this book, it was clear to me that I came across as old school. But old school can be referred to people fairly new to the industry too, for example a door supervisor who is referred to as having old school tendencies and who works to the ways of us longer serving doormen.

So what are the old school ways of working? Is it the stereotypical drag someone into the alleyway and give them a real good licking? Is it displaying a terrible attitude? Is it going to work to shag as many girls as you can? Maybe it is, but probably only in the eyes of the uneducated people who have had one or two bad experiences with door supervisors who have treated them badly. I hate seeing programs on TV – like Bouncers – where people are interviewed in the street saying bouncers are all wankers, cunts, baby killers etc. Well we are not. Believe it or not some are very well educated, take Andi who appeared with me in Bouncers, he is a secondary school teacher. I also have my teaching qualifications but I teach anyone over 16 years of age as opposed to secondary school age, and I teach all types of courses including door supervision, close protection, security guarding, CCTV, health & safety, fire awareness and a vast array of employability courses to get the unemployed back into work. I also work on the door with a very good new school doorman with strong old school ways of working who during the day works for the county council and is responsible for the care of the elderly and all matters concerning social services where he makes decisions that change people's lives for the better.

So how far back does the term old school stretch? I recently asked a customer this when he said he remembered me being on the door "back in the day" and he described me to his mate as old school, to which he told me that because he remembered me being on the door at The Hippodrome I am seen as old school. I worked at the Hippodrome between 1994 and 1997 so to him that is old school, but to me it isn't because in my mind I am still working and despite me having breaks in working regular, I am still working as an active doorman and therefore I see 1994 as still part of me now, but the reality is working in 1994 was totally different to working in 2014.

So what is the difference between old school and new school? Basically two different eras of time where there is a big difference in the ways of working practically and the ways we have to work academically. Let me start with the latter – academically; we all know that now we have to sit through a training course, pass exams, apply to the SIA for a licence for which we have to pay a non-refundable fee for and then hope that nothing untoward pops up on a criminal record check that will delay our application. I talk in depth later on about the training so I won't go into too much detail here, however just briefly included in the course is first aid awareness, fire awareness, how to deal with emergencies, report writing and vulnerable people both adults and children as anyone under the age of 18 is legally a child and of course under 18's do get in venues and we have to be taught about looking after their welfare.

The exams we take are at a level 2 multiple choice and the industry standard pass mark is 70%, and you have to sit the exams yourself in controlled exam conditions having proven your identity. You are not able to get your mate Big Dave to sit the exams for you, or are you able to refer to reference books or your mobile phone with access to the internet for help. Now although the course is not hard, and as I explain later a good tutor will pack out their training with experiences, discussions and real life scenarios, you must attend all the guided contact hours to be able to sit the exam, so again you can't send Big Dave in your place.

As for working practically this has had a big knock on effect from the academic side of things as the new school or doormen are learning their trade in the classroom before even getting into the pubs and clubs. When I started in 1990 the question was more or less "can you fight?" and if you answered "yes" then you got a job on the door. It didn't matter if you had a criminal record, or if you could not write a report out, it really was a case of getting to work with a stash of weaponry to hand either on your person or hidden in the club. I make no secret of the fact that in the past I have carried a knuckle duster and a bottle of Vick's Sinex nasal spray with the Sinex liquid removed and replaced with ammonia in order to protect myself, however I never actually used either and then I only carried such items when I started at a new club and didn't know if the new doormen I was working with would back me up. As a funny side track on this note, I came home one day from my day job and my poor Mum, who had been ill, was sitting in the chair looking worse than she had the day before. I asked if she was ok and she said she felt rough as anything with a headache and blocked sinuses, but she had found my Sinex and give that a shot but it made her feel worse.

Fuck me she had only squirted ammonia up both nostrils so no wonder she felt worse! Nowadays I would not dare carry anything not just because its illegal but because I can't jeapardise my position as a security industry teacher by teaching students the legal side of the job and then that night arm myself with a duster and ammonia to go to work.

I see big differences in the mix of old school and new school doormen when I am at work either for the company I work for or for the other companies. New school doormen work for the company, they are keen to impress, keen to earn themselves more shifts, willing to travel long distances from home to clock up a CV packed with lots and lots of different venues where they have worked. However what with me being old school I am not into all that shit. I will be totally honest with you I just want to earn a few extra quid and if I can walk round the corner and work at Fashion Café in Colchester I will do that rather than drive and waste my fuel to travel to Clacton to cover for the head doorman at The Liquor Lounge if he has a night off. That's just me, and I cannot speak for any other doorman or woman here, but I am not out to impress anyone, I have no need to 'make a name' for myself and show the company I am good at my job. Michael who was on Bouncers with me as the boss of the company I work for knows that too and as I am his longest serving doorman I get given the right by him to pick and choose where and when I work.

That comes with time. Time that new school doormen don't have. At the same time I don't take the piss to demand where I work and if I am required to work somewhere far away then I will, however my choice is not to if I can help it. Fashion Café is an ideal place for me to work, it is walking distance from my house and despite Aykut the owner not being the easiest person to work for I have known him for about 20 years and can handle him and his working ways. In 1997 I left The Colchester Hippodrome and went to work for Regency Security Services in Chelmsford, at a time when I was still fairly new to the industry and also new to a company I had no right to demand or request where to work and did travel about Essex to fill shifts for them despite sometimes having to travel 30, 40, 50 miles from home.

Would you get me travelling those distances now to work? To quote a favourable phrase of mine "you can go fuck off" would be my response now, however I can assure you if Halle Berry was doing an appearance at the venue I would be there in a fucking flash, but other than that no. So that could be seen as a defining difference between the two eras of working. Years ago I would have driven those miles to prove to the company or the venue that I was a good and willing worker, however now I won't.

Old School doormen and women are set in their ways whereas the new school are educated in their ways. It's sometimes hard for me being in the two eras as I work in the old school ways but teach the new school ways, but I must admit you will very rarely see me doing any of the new school ways myself when at work. Allow me to list some of the things I do and what the new school would probably do;

- You ask me to search someone and I will delegate that piss boring job. Do you think I want to wrap my arms round some big fat smelly drunken twat who breaths all over me? Bollocks am I. But the new school doormen do and they do it because they are willing to show they are a valuable asset to the venue. It is a very important part of the security function but I will opt out of doing that before I even start having to bring 4 tonne of hand sanatiser to work.

- I will iron my shirt 5 seconds before I wear it and then I only iron the bit that is visible to the customers – to basically the 'V' from neck down to chest. I couldn't give a shit what is not seen under my jacket or coat but years ago I had the smartest, crispest starched shirts on the door. If you are lucky I may even wash the shirt rather than Fabreze it…. ha ha I am joking here on the washing part but couldn't resist that to which someone probably was thinking "dirty bastard".

- I will wear my SIA licence around my neck with the lanyard the SIA themselves provide. I refuse to wear one of those armband things that most people wear now. The conditions of your licence say it must be visible and I comply with that, give me a stupid fucking armband and unfortunately everyone you give me will break when I try to put it on my arm. I did wear one for the photo shoot of Bouncers on my last shift at The Liquor Lounge but that was under protest I can tell you. New school doorman all seem wear them like some medal which does make me laugh as recently there was a Facebook group called 'Doormen Wankers' that was fucking hilarious with all the new school doormen posing with their armbands on.

- I will still uphold the old school traditions that if someone is rude to me or displays a bad attitude then they do not come in. I have worked with a lot of new school doormen who seem to allow this direct piss taking to happen and then allow the customers in which goes against everything we stand for as the security of the venue. If a customer can take the piss at the front door and get away with it the chances are they will take the piss inside the venue because it is obviously clear they have no respect for the door team. I can see through all the bollocks people give you when they want to get in a venue by saying they "respect me" and "I promise I will behave" after I have said they can't come in when they have been rude.

- I am not worried about losing my licence when someone is about to attack me or offer violence towards me, as I never was overly worried about being arrested years ago before the SIA was around. It is because I have always taken an interest in the UK Law and the fact that every UK citizen has the right to defend themselves legally, even when at work and when at work as a door supervisor. Just because we are in the forefront of the security industry it does not mean we are exempt from this ruling and therefore we can defend ourselves even if this means using the pre-emptive strike. New school doormen are worried about losing their licence and I have seen them hold back and either get hurt or their colleagues get hurt. I am not advocating violence here and I hate the bully door supervisors that go looking for trouble just to have a fight, however at the same time some of the new school – not all – but some of them need to 'grow a set' and understand that they do not have to take abuse from the customers.

Let me talk a bit about what I mean in my last point above about new school door supervisors needing to 'grow a set'. New school door supervisors need to understand this is a violent profession and just doing a course because the job centre sent you, or you do the course because it makes you look good walking around with your SIA badge in your wallet so you can tell people you are a doorman will not stand you in good stead when and if you go to work. I do actually have a lot of time for the job centre trained people despite me reading on internet forums many posts slagging them off, because I have trained hundreds of them and they are not all bad. Some people have fell on hard times through no fault of their own, been sent on an 'employment' course by the job centre and included within that is the door supervisor qualification. 90% of the people I train on these courses will never ever go and work on the door doing what I have done for over 24 years, however they will end up with the same qualification as I have and technically can stand side by side with me and work.

The majority of them simply want to get back to work and opt for a security course as they see themselves working in a warehouse or building site or corporate security but it's the training companies that put these people through a door supervisor course as it gives the students the extra chance of employment as a security guard or a door supervisor. That said, I have trained a lot of good people this way who have gone on to make very good door supervisors and who have had their life turned around by attending a course I gave them on a job centre programme.

It's the wannabes that really make my shit itch and it's these people that I refer to above, the idiot that does a course and then flashes his badge about saying he is a doorman. Is he fuck a doorman, he's a badge holder, or shirt filler as is often referred to them and he isn't worth a wank. I carry my SIA badge in my wallet because I hold a Close Protection licence and when I am working in that role I keep my licence on me and available should I be asked to produce it.

What I do not do is walk around with my Door Supervisor licence in my wallet and flash it to everyone saying I am a doorman and try to gain entry to other people's clubs based on the fact that I have a badge. One idiot from Colchester who I will not name arrived at my door one night and flashed his badge right in my face saying he was eligible for free entry and that he worked for Michael. Funny that because I am his longest serving doorman and I had never seen this prick before, so I politely refused him free entry and made him queue up. If he had approached me, introduced himself, shook my hand and had a conversation then I may have helped him but he didn't and therefore I did not offer him the respect any other well-mannered SIA badge holder would have got from me with a proper approach. As it turns out this particular waste of space still struts around Colchester telling everyone he is a doorman and apparently he has on many times said he is going to beat me up, however I am still in one piece, I never see him and when he has rarely worked on the door as a stand-in and its kicked off he is nowhere to be seen, so I don't think I need to hire my own Close Protection team just yet.

New school doormen as I have said are educated in their ways as directed from the learning outcomes of the SIA. That is not a bad thing, in fact I am from the bread of people that think the SIA is a good scheme and has assisted the industry to a certain extent, but the problem was they did jump in head first and upset the industry when first introduced. No one likes change and that was the problem when the old school doormen had to suddenly attend a course and have their criminal record checked before they could do the job most of them had done for years. The problem now with the SIA is the fact that is has produced the new school breed where anyone can go off and do the course, get a door supervisor licence and as I have said earlier suddenly call themselves a doorman or doorwoman. Now you may think if they are not up to the standard required to work in real life, they will not get work but because of the Private Security Industry Act 2001 it is illegal for anyone to employ people without a valid licence, therefore people with a licence are in some cases like rocking horse shit and it doesn't initially matter if they are any good, it all goes on if they have a badge, and if they do they will get work. Gone are the old school days of when a venue was short us doormen would ring up our mate and tell them to get a shirt on and start at 9pm, gone are the days of finding out someone is shit and sacking them on the spot and you again ring your mate to start the following night, now you can't do that so much as any replacement must have a badge. There is eventually in time going to be a complete transition whereby every single person working in the security industry only knows the SIA scheme and never ever worked before it was introduced. How will the industry be then?

I can't answer that with an answer that everyone would agree with, but what I can do is answer with my opinion and that is that unless the new school door supervisors adopt old school mentality whilst still maintaining their new school training and staying within the Law and SIA codes of practice then the industry will become a joke. Before everyone now gets onto social media to abuse me, let me explain my answer because I have thought about this for a while. New school doormen need to realise that what you learn on a course is the basics of the job and its set in a classroom with no real life training. If you go out to work with the worry that as soon as you say or do something you will lose your licence then why on earth did you bother training in the first place? You would be better suited selling eggs down the market than standing on a door dealing with the abuse. I fully agree the old school bully 'bouncer' needed to be eradicated from the industry, however when the SIA was introduced I really thought our wages would increase, but all they have done is go down. 1990 my nightly wage was £75 cash in my hand when I was 18 years old and knew fuck all, now it's £12.50 an hour, PAYE and I do at most 4½ hours a night making £56.25 before tax with all my experience and ability. Admittedly the scope of the industry for someone at my level now is far better than it probably would have been if I was 42 in 1990 because now I could apply for a job at a big security company and probably work quite comfortably in an area manager's role earning £45,000 a year. But with what I said about the industry becoming a joke, why would I take that position when I could see most of the people working under me are new school doormen who don't work how I used to when I was their age. I am one person, I cannot change the whole of the UK's new school doormen into working like us old school doormen did or still do.

My idea of the industry becoming a joke is not meant in a detrimental way, it is my own opinion that I have developed over the years based on what I have seen coming through my training rooms. I feel it's the mentality that is lacking not the physical presence of big hulking bodybuilders or champion boxers, which is why I feel it is this failing that could turn the industry into a joke. I seriously hope not, but without the old school ways being passed down or the new school doormen being 'brain washed' that they cannot defend themselves, or they can't touch a person because it is an assault then I worry.

Chapter Six

What's it really Like?

In order to give you an insight into what it's like working on the door, I shall explain to you some of the events that have happened to me and how I felt at the time and what I went through. Some were good, fun times whereas some were not. My accounts of working on the door may differ from other experienced doormen and women out there, however I am sure anyone reading this will relate to a lot of what I say.

So, what is it really like? What is it really like to get paid for being in a nightclub, a pub or an event full of young girls, young pretty girls who flirt with you and make you feel really good about yourself... it's fantastic. It's fantastic until your awareness of the girls and not of your colleagues causes someone to get hurt, and invariably it isn't you getting hurt but someone you should have been keeping an eye on. In the world of doorwork this is called 'watching the back' of your mates.

I would rather stand on the door with a doorman or doorwoman who will be looking out for me, who would if the shit hit the fan be there with me side by side fighting until we were both beaten. You will not last long in this industry if you get a bad reputation for letting the team down, you need to be there for your colleagues and be switched on and alert to what is around you. By that I do not mean nor want any of you reading this to become a bully and suddenly think you are 'it' and have to prove to everyone around you that you can fight, or you can push someone out a door so they end up in a heap on the path and make them look like a fool. Anyone in the world can launch a drunk off their feet, and that sort of behaviour from doormen really pisses me off.

In the 90's when I was head doorman of the Colchester Hippodrome the story was different. I was 22 years old when I started working there, and prior to that I had been working regular at another club in the town that had closed down following the murder of a young soldier outside the club. Back then the leisure industry was different to today with pubs having to shut at 11pm leaving everyone pouring out the pubs to head off to a nightclub where they would spend the rest of the evening. In Colchester at the time there was only a handful of nightclubs open until 2am, with the Hippodrome being the biggest, the most glamourous club slap bang in the middle of the High Street.

When I started our uniform was dinner suit, wing collared shirt with a bow tie, with the customers all having to be in smart clothes, the males in particular had to be in trousers, shoes with a smart shirt, and it wasn't too long before I started that all male customers had to wear a tie! About 10 months after I started at the club, the legendary head doorman Ian

Mckelly, God rest his soul, left having ran the door since the club had opened in 1988. We had a new manager Steve, God rest his soul too, who installed Big Les as head doorman however after a short time Les left and I was made head doorman at the age of 23. Suddenly I was thrust into the role of running a team of doormen numbering at most 15 a night, in the biggest club in the town, 1,295 capacity which was packed almost every one of the 4 nights we opened and in a town housing one of the country's biggest Army barracks. Everything ran smoothly for a few months, however I don't mind admitting I was out of my depth, but I have never been one for giving up or shirking responsibility so I started to settle into the job and build a team of doormen and doorwomen around me.

I had to learn quickly the finer aspects of the job, but with it came a new found problem that hit me like a ton of bricks.

I started hearing through the town's grapevine that people were saying I was too young to be in charge of the Hippodrome and that I was there to be 'taken down' resulting in me suddenly finding myself coming under attack from people wanting to get a name for themselves by bashing me up. This I found strange as I wasn't putting myself up on a pedestal nor was I at this time acting in a way whereby I was pissing people off. I simply took over the reins from Ian and Les whereby I refused to let in all the scum of the town who had previously been banned for fighting or drugs. I think because in such a short period of time both Ian and then Les had left, the scum of the town assumed I did not know who they were and they could come in. The problem you have with people who I label scum is they only know one language and that is not the nicely nicely language either, it really is the 'hit them fucking hard first then ask questions later' approach.

To be totally honest with you I am afraid that is probably still the case today with anyone of that nature, however back in the 90's there was less CCTV surveillance around and people would literally turn up at the front door and cause a fight with either me or my door team on the front door with me. I was aware a little bit of the law back then and I was quite up to speed with the knowledge of the self-defence rule and the rule where by you can hit first to prevent yourself becoming a victim, so I put up a very big mental protective barrier around myself and literally started to consider everyone a threat who came too close to me.

Looking back now that may have been the wrong approach because it did bring on a fair bit of trouble for me, but I had to protect my staff by not letting the utter scum in the club. I have a philosophy when I am working as a head doorman and that is that if anyone is going to get hit, if anyone is going to get hurt in a night's work then that will be me and not my staff. I will put myself in the way of trouble to protect my staff even if I know my arse is crapping itself, I am outnumbered and I can see a very painful ending in sight for my face.

The Hippodrome at the time was owned and operated by Rank Leisure and they decided to move Steve the manager and we ended up with Martin as the new manager, sadly again God rest his soul. Suddenly the club changed direction, some say for the better, some say for the worse. I was in two minds as to the changes Martin brought in because on one hand he brought the dance scene to Colchester and the music now being played was exactly the sort of music I love, however with it came a lot of drug use, mainly cocaine and ecstasy.

This brought with it massive problems between me and my door team and a different clientele coming in from London with their drugs which we were finding more and more during entry searches and from blatant use in the toilets. I decided to install two doormen constantly walking the club as a pair to combat the drug use, Martin 'the doorman' as we called him (to differentiate between him and the manager) and Archer a big body builder originally from Devon. They worked well as a team, Martin from gypsy background who was game as anything and Archer the big muscle man who could literally pick up a man and walk them out the door with their feet dangling. Whenever they called me down to the toilet area following a drug find I would make my way to the toilets with the butterflies in my stomach churning, wondering what the fuck I would be walking into.

Normally it would end up being a friend of the DJs, or promoters, or even people saying they were friends of Martin the manager even though Martin didn't know them. Everyone knows the manager in this industry! So, what with my zero tolerance on drugs I opted to remove the people from the venue despite who they said they know, having explained to them the consequences if they refused to leave peacefully. These consequences would have been to call the police and have them arrested, something I was not keen to action as I would rather the person leave and never come back. However a lot of the time these people refused to leave peacefully and a fight would be put up by the people high on drugs, or as I was finding rather quickly, people looked down on me being younger than them and saw my young age as a weakness.

I have never been one for 'bigging' myself up because I am well aware that there is always someone out there bigger and harder than me, however I did work in the way that no one would take advantage of me no matter how big they were or how hard they snarled at me. As a result of this I got myself into a fair bit of trouble with local gangs, London based gangs and the local police, with me being arrested 4 times during 1996 all for accusations of ABH, GBH and violence stemming from drug related incidents. During one of my interviews on Channel 4's Bouncers series I mentioned if you don't control the drug problem in a club then it will over run you. I based that comment on the experiences I had at the Hippodrome and the events that happened in that club during its dance scene period when Martin was manager.

After being head doorman for about a year I seemed to be pissing off every unsavoury character in Colchester, Ipswich which was the next big town up the A12, and the odd drug dealer from London. The London problem was becoming more of an issue in 1995-96, with a lot more people travelling up to visit the club when we had certain promotions on. On one particular night the doormen caught a bloke with a very large amount of cocaine on him all wrapped up and ready to sell. I cannot recall how many wraps he had but it was just enough for the police to be called. As I have previously stated I was not in favour of calling the police all the time, but more in favour of getting the drugs off the street, bag them, record it and place them in the safe in the office upstairs. We would then ask the person or persons to leave the club and never return. On this occasion we had no choice, mainly because I was not going to explain to the police why we had bagged up a massive amount of cocaine and not called them. So the police were called, arrested the bloke and took the details of the doormen involved, however they did not take my name. A few weeks later Martin the manager called us all upstairs into the office before the club opened and played us a voicemail on the club's landline.

This voicemail sent shivers down my spine as it was a direct threat towards me for getting his dealer arrested, and a warning that I should leave the club. I was not named in the voicemail but I was referred to as the head doorman, so Martin the manager advised me to go home for a few weeks but I refused and I defiantly took up my position on the front door. Martin instructed the other doormen to never leave me alone and that none of us should travel in to work alone because he was worried for my safety.

I tried to dismiss this threat because over the few years prior I had been threatened with all sorts of violence, retribution and even one of my doormen Mick who was similar size to me being attacked and stabbed outside his own home in what turned out to be a mistaken attack intended for me. So one night a few weeks after this threat was made to me, I was stood on the High Street of Colchester outside the front door of the Hippodrome talking to my best mate Wayne who worked with me at the club. Suddenly Wayne stopped talking and went completely white and stared at me, and shouted for me to get in the club. Wondering what the fuck was going on I dismissed him and asked him what he was going in about. He then informed me a red laser dot had appeared on my forehead right between my eyes, and immediately I shit myself and legged it back into the door of the club waiting for the assassin's bullet to ram into the door. A very nervous Wayne followed me and we waited there trying to locate the source of the laser, until – funnily now looking back – a mate of mine who was a taxi driver, got out of his taxi parked on the rank opposite the club, shouted and waved at me... with his laser pen. The fear he had unknowingly installed into me will to this day always live with me. That sort of thing can never ever be taught to you in a classroom on a 4 day course. I don't care what any other tutor tells you, or what extra courses you go on which are designed to prepare you for working, nothing in the world has ever scared me as much as that and I defy any classroom situation to replicate that.

Being threatened in the line of your work is legally unacceptable under the Health & Safety at Work Act 1974 as your employer must put measures in place to make you safe while at work whether you are employed directly by them or self-employed. When working on the door we are in a nightclub, or pub, or at a music festival or any other event that people attend socially, however it is still our place of work and must be treated as such.

So when you get threatened, verbally abused or attacked then in theory you should be protected from this. The reality is it happens, you will get abused and anyone who goes into this industry blinkered that it won't happen to you needs a reality check. You will walk around your venue with this whacking great big target on your back, you are what I call 'in the public eye' where everybody sees what you do – good and bad. You can do 99 good things and no one will bat an eye lid, but do one thing wrong and everyone sees it, talks about it or worse still films it on their mobile phones and in minutes it's up on social media for the whole world to see. There was a video circulating on Facebook earlier this year where a doorman got involved in a fight with a customer out on the street and after a bit of grappling and fighting the doorman picked up the customer and slammed him down onto his back whereby you heard the sickening sound of head and body against the pavement. My initial thought was "Fuck me he is in trouble", but after watching it again and taking into account that all we saw on Facebook was the actual fight, how do we know what abuse and threats that doorman had had to put up with? Yes in the normal situation his actions are bang out of order, unprofessional and not acceptable from door supervisors. But let's now imagine that perhaps, just maybe that customer had threatened to stab the doorman, and the doorman had put up with this for a fair length of time, acted professionally and kept his cool until the customer made a move towards him. Whether that customer had a knife or not, that doorman was not to know that and therefore by law if he has an honest held belief that he is in danger, he can defend himself and do whatever he feels in necessary to avert that danger, with any action he takes being reasonable in the circumstances.

So now let's relook at the video again, and look at it that the doorman fighting with the customer is fighting to save his life because he has been threatened with being stabbed. Sounds drastic, but that is how you must look at it. Knives kill, end of. My whole point of this little paragraph is that as a doorman you can be acting totally legally and within your UK rights of law, however the bystanders' film you doing the bad stuff and whack it up on social media.

The most harrowing event that happened to me resulted in myself being attacked and hospitalised by 12 other men at the front door of the Hippodrome in 1996. Just prior to the attack I had been for an interview and got offered a job at a nightclub in Brentwood and was on the verge of handing my notice in, but before I could do so, I had a fight in the club and the retribution from family members of the man I fought with occurred within 30 minutes and was talked about around Colchester for years. But from my point of view I had a bigger talking point to consider. What would people think of me if I now took up the higher paid job in Brentwood so soon after being attacked on my front door? It played on my mind that I would be seen as a bottler, or had run away from what happened to me, so I had to stay at the Hippodrome.

I had to stay even though the club was becoming a very rough and violent place to work because of the ever increasing drug problem which unbeknown to me was stemming from people above Martin the manager so as fast as we were catching people, they were getting 'inside assistance' to carry on. It got to the point where I would hate going in at 8.30pm and the sight of the clock saying 2.30am was the best thing in the world, we were literally fighting every night sometimes 3, 4, 5 big fights a night.

And then I bumped into David. David was a feared man around Colchester and bordered on the wrong side of the law despite his brother Michael running a successful security company in the town. David was a very loyal brother when it came down to family but very much his own person when it came to flouncing the law, often bringing trouble his brother's way without Michael knowing until something happened, as in our case.

The main toilets at the Hippodrome were downstairs, under street level of the High Street but on street level of the street to the side of the club due to a big inclined hill. One Friday night the toilets were blocked and we had to call a drainage firm in to rod them clear, so I placed a doorman on the open side door to stop people coming in. I had never let David in the club due to past fights he had had with the doormen, but somehow David took his chance and blagged his way in. To this day I do not know if he sneaked in the side door, got in the front door when I was not there or was let in another way, all I know is while I was having a quick walk around the club I bumped into him at the side doors. The side doors were a big double skinned fire escape doors situated off the dance floor and led into the side street and a block of flats. I stopped David and asked how he got in and reaffirmed that he is not welcome in the club and had to leave. I was stood with the fire doors on my left hand side and David was stood to my left with his back to them, so we were facing across each other. I can't recall what David said but next thing I saw was his trademark head-butt flying towards my face, so I took one step back and threw the cleanest of right hooks I have ever thrown.

David flew backwards against the fire doors and the momentum of his body caused him to open the push bar and fall into the street unconscious. I remember shoving his legs out the door and closed the door quickly to get back up the front door before he came round in a rage. But he did not come. After 5 or so minutes I sent my number 2 in command Norman to have a look and he said that David was just coming round and stumbling up the hill towards the High Street, so I prepared myself for round 2 but it did not come. Norman and I then resumed normal proceedings at the front door while I told the management what had happened at the side door. Moments later I stepped down off the front door to look up and down the street and when I looked left I saw Michael walking towards me. I remember saying to Norman "hello, Michael is steaming up to see us", I didn't see the other 11 behind him until they were right on top of me.

That was it, goodnight. Michael smashed me a right hook into my face and my legs went, and I slipped on the steps of the front door and I immediatly realised the power of the punch as I had pissed myself. What happened next I have no memory of at all, except I came round in the reception of the club curled up being kicked and punched while I could hear the receptionist screaming, before I heard Michael shouting "he's had enough", resulting in everyone then leaving the club. The scene that was left was total destruction because the mob had smashed up reception as well as me.

I was helped to my feet by people around me and taken up to the office along with Norman who had also received a beating. Rachel the deputy manager called an ambulance for me and Norman and we were taken off for treatment, where unbeknown to us at the time David was being treated in A&E at the same time for the injuries I initially caused him.

The after effects from this attack on me were delayed because a week later I passed out and was sent to Broomfield Hospital in Chelmsford for tests on my brain. I had to regularly attend the doctors and hospital for years and for quite a while was on medication to control my mood swings and violent outbursts toward people around me that I loved. My then girlfriend unfortunately taking the full force of my mood swings, not that I was ever violent towards her, but I was so argumentative and needed help. She did a lot for me in terms of researching brain injuries and helping me with my short term memory loss which was becoming more and more apparent and frustrating for me.

I couldn't even remember simple things like what a table was called, what a pen was and worse still my son's own name. These memory losses were not all the time, just periodically, however the help she got for me put me back into normality. Despite what went on between her and I, in years to follow she did a lot for me and my head injury with just simply understanding and being patient. Without her help I can honestly say I think I would of ended up being a very violent and short tempered man.

Now for the twist in fate, the postscript to the whole event. The following night after the attack I called Michel up to the Hippodrome for a chat with me over what had happened. Michael arrived after both our respective clubs had shut and we went to the office for a chat and to look though the CCTV footage of the incident between me and David. In the office were me and Norman, Martin the manager, Michael, his business partner John and our peacekeeper Big Steve, a very well-liked and former doorman friend of everyone. The story that David had told Michael when he stumbled into him after I hit him causing his nose to literally break and be positioned at 90^0 to his face, was that me and all the doormen had given him a kicking. Michael seeing his brother all bashed up, and thinking it's a Friday and Ryder will be mobb handed with doormen decided to get a firm up to confront us.

Michael admitted that he had no idea what to say to me as he was walking up to the door and at that moment he felt the best thing was to knock me out. We played Michael the CCTV footage and from the moment David threw the head-butt to me closing the fire door was 4 seconds. Michael looked shocked and stood in disbelief suddenly realising that only I had caused the damage to David, all within a matter of seconds, and not all the doorman as David had said. We all stood talking and Michael realised the attack upon me was uncalled for that night, he apologised profusely and we all shook hands. I remember Michael saying he thought my face would have been more heavily marked, little did I or he know the damage inside my head which I have already mentioned.

So, where did this event go from here? The police wanted me to make a statement against Michael and everyone else who attacked me but I refused. As a result my application for a new Council run scheme of licensing door supervisors introduced in 1996 was suspended for this reason and it took me a lengthy appeal process to have it granted. Michael and I kept an amicable peace despite me constantly receiving threats from wankers who were friends of David, including David himself attempting again to get in the club and then harassing my girlfriend at work. I eventually left the Hippodrome in 1997 and went to work in Chelmsford, however in March of 1999 I was more or less head hunted and recruited to work at a dance nightclub in Clacton called Rumours, where I impressed that much I was made head doorman. Who ran the door security company? Michael. I have now worked constantly for Michael since that date and we are best of friends. I made my peace with David years ago, with him very ashamed of his actions towards my girlfriend. David and I are also good friends now, to the point where on one occasion in Clacton I found myself separated from my door team alone at the front door and as usual the fucking radio had packed up.

I stood facing a group of London holiday makers about to kick off and out the corner of my eye I saw this man appear and wink at me. It was David and he calmly walked up, stood beside me and the group backed off. We very rarely speak about the night at the Hippodrome because its old history now, but the effects are still with me. I have trouble clearing my throat, I have trouble swallowing sometimes and I still suffer from the odd banging headache all stemming from the head injury I suffered that night.

Over the years working I have had some side splitting laughs, and I can say that because when you still laugh about them 10, 15, 20 years later then I know for a fact with my sense of humour then I would have been crying at the time of the event. My best mate Wayne and I have worked together at virtually every club since the Hippodrome days, and although Wayne no longer works the door we still have childish giggles when we think of funny events. We used to have this mutual understanding of what the other was going to do when it came to messing about and relieving the boredom that does creep up on you sometimes on a cold boring night. Wayne has this certain thing that makes him piss himself laughing no matter where he is or what mood he may be in… food droppers. The amusement Wayne has seeing a drunk spend ages attempting to eat food only to then drop the lot on the floor has caused him to virtually cry with laughter. I have always had the same laughter at drunks, but Wayne takes it that bit further with his obvious enjoyment at other people's misfortune. One night both Wayne and I were working at the Silk Road in Colchester and unbeknown to the poor lad in question he satisfied both myself and Wayne's enjoyment at his drunken food antics.

A big lad, clearly shit faced was stumbling down Queen Street with a tray of food. He then decided that trying to walk down the hill of the Street, being drunk and eating was too much to handle so he leant against the window of the Silk Road and attempted to eat his food with most of it going down his top. I could see Wayne starting to giggle, which set me off which in turn made the drunk lad attempt more and more to put the food in his mouth with some sort of sobriety. This was making Wayne worse which was making me worse which was making the drunk try harder. Got the picture? Next thing the drunk lad loses his footing, starts to fall down the hill while trying to remain upright just as he tries to put food in his mouth... picture a human Leaning Tower of Pizza. Bang.... he hits the floor like a felled tree, fucking food flies everywhere up the window of the club, all over his face and clothes. Me and Wayne are crying, we cannot stand up for laughing. After a while we started to calm down and then the realisation that the lad had obviously knocked himself out came across so we called an ambulance for him, which fortunately arrived quite quickly. Out step two female paramedics to attend to him, and they decide he needs to go to hospital as no one could really say how hard he hit his head to knock himself out. Myself and Wayne still had the childish fit of giggles from the image of him keeling over, and when the paramedics asked us to assist moving him we helped out, still trying not to laugh. The paramedics had asked if me and Wayne could grip his belt with one hand and the ankle of his trousers with the other while they supported his head. So we all got into position ready to lift him onto the stretcher, and as we lifted his fucking trousers ripped and came away like some clown's performance trousers. Well that was it, me and Wayne were again crying with laughter and could do no more than to walk off bent over with stomach ache and tears rolling down our face.

I have lost count over the years of all the troubles, threats, fights and laughs I have had. I have worked with some utter shite doormen who are not worth a wank, but then again I have worked with some doormen and doorwomen who would quite literally put their life on the line to back you up. One that I cannot go without mentioning is 'Stormin Norman the Doorman' or 'Normski' as we used to call him. Norman stood side by side with me when I was attacked at the Hippodrome, nothing to do with my altercation with David at all but still took a beating along with me rather than leave me on my own. None of the other doormen working that night could assist anyway as there was no time at all to call for assistance and the whole event in the reception that night was over in no more than a minute.

Norman is one of the funniest blokes you could ever meet, and has the ability to turn anything into a laugh. One occasion I stood at the front door at the end of the night giving out fliers with Norman and this bloke walked up to take one out of Norm's hand and looked up to say thank you. He then stopped dead having clocked Norman's face and then went into one at him for selling him a dodgy motor. Another one of Norman's nicknames was Honest Norm or The Teflon Don due to his dodgy dealing in the murky world of second hand car sales, and this poor bloke had bought a prized motor off Norman. We all used to wind Norman up about his car dealings to the point where we started calling Theresa his wife, Marleen after Boycie's wife in Only Fools and Horses. This particular situation at the front door was becoming more and more comical as Norman had this tendency to make these funny bodily movements side to side when he was being mischievous, and after a while he would then start moving his head up to sort of pull his neck up and out of his collared shirt, bit like a well to do country gent. The bloke was going potty at Norman about the pile of shit he had sold him and all Norm kept saying was "sold as seen son, sold as seen. No warranty given", to which the bloke then said that he was going down the motorway and the fucking steering wheel came off in his hand at 80mph. Well yet again there was me curled up in the corner laughing my bollocks off.

There was also the occasion when Norman had upset someone, god knows who, but obviously one of the more unsavoury characters of the town. Norman used to drive around in some of the cars he was selling and for a while was using a black mini as his transport to and from the club. Eventually he sold it to some poor bastard who while sitting in rush hour traffic somewhere in Colchester got literally pulled out the car by a group of blokes and bashed up with a shovel... clearly a beating meant for Norman!

I can't end this chapter without talking about girls. Any girls reading this wanting to get into door work then please forgive me for writing this bit from a male's point of view but I can only speak from experience myself of having girls chat me up and fortunately not men. Doorgirls do get a lot of attention from men too, but it goes without saying some girls are attracted to doormen. Other than the mother of my two eldest kids who I went to school with, I have met virtually all my girlfriends and my ex-wife through working on the door. Girls do throw themselves at you and distract you as I said at the start of this chapter and you should never allow them to come between you and your work. But let's be honest, countless numbers of relationships happen at work and you will be working in an environment where people go out to socialise and ultimately pull. Some of the girls I have met I have had long term relationships with, and as I said I met my wife while I was working and remained with her for 5 years. I am now in a very happy long term relationship with Kim and I too met her on the door, however she was working opposite TP's in Colchester when she caught my eye, as Kim was a doorgirl at Route Nightclub on Colchester's notorious Queen Street and we met across the 'Gaza Strip' or 'Baghdad Alley' as Queen Street is known in Colchester. So just a word of warning, my old boxing trainer many years ago used to tell us "women weaken legs. You get distracted at home, get a bunk up and ya legs get weak and you get knocked out". Girls in a nightclub environment are dangerous when you are working so lads keep your eyes on your colleagues and save the bunk ups for after work.

Chapter Seven

A modern Day Bouncers Role

You can ask one hundred different people what the modern day Bouncers or Door Supervisors role is and I would bet that at least 75% of people would say something on the lines of 'Throwing People out of Bars", "Beating People Up" or "Jumping into Fights". So what do you think a modern day Bouncers role is? If you agree with the 75% of people above then I am sorry but you're not cut-out to be a Bouncer, Doorman, Door Supervisor or whatever you would like to call it.

Times have changed and the job has changed so much, almost beyond recognition some way for the better and some ways for the worse but no matter what you think the days of Bouncers taking someone round to the back ally and beating the shit out of them or gone! It's not all about violence, either combating it or dishing it out its so much more than that in this day and age no matter what stereotypes are still on us.

In this day and age what's expected of Door Staff does differ from venue to venue but on the whole, across the board a large part of the role is now customer service focused, front of house management. Yes its still ejecting drunks, its still knocking back underage kids from getting in the methods expected have changed, it all about your verbal skills and body language.

Contrary to the way action films portray bouncers, professional club security is about avoiding conflict, not engaging in it, quality security people are level headed, perceptive, and very good at sensing and defusing conflict situations before they escalate or even start. Nightclubs in particular are frequently filled with sexual tension and intoxicated people, and they require experienced professionals to keep things under control.

The first staff member of most venues that the customer comes into contact with is the doorman and as we all know that first contact can portray the image of all other contact and of the business or venue itself and have a huge effect on the customer experience, and let's face it that's what it's all about these days, customer experience and making them want to come back. A huge part of today's role is checking IDs to confirm that everyone entering the venue is of legal age, this needs an eye for detail and a sixth sense if you like. With so many fake widely ID's available these days its an area that requires you to have your wits about you.

Also barring entry to intoxicated people and people who are known to have caused trouble in the past and to uphold the venues rules, such as dress code is a big thing. Its about stopping potential trouble and conflict before it happens these days rather than dealing with it when it does, so if a punter looks like they will cause trouble or have had too much to drink, or seem like they are under the influence of drugs then you don't let them enter in the first place. Often you can just tell after you have some experience on the Door, nothing you can put your finger on but you just know that this person who wants to get into your bar is bother. Remember its you that will have to take them out if trouble does start so as I always say, what's the point of letting them in only to throw them out?

The doorman can make a crucial contribution to the security of the club by keeping out people who might cause problems, thus saving the inside staff the trouble of dealing with them. Doormen need to be good judges of character and very tactful in their dealings with people. Bouncers will also patrol a bar and dance floor to keep an eye on things. Their job is to sense trouble developing before it gets out of hand, and to take steps to defuse it. This may mean having a word with an unruly customer, stopping alcohol being served to someone who is becoming excessively drunk, or heading off a conflict between two or more customers.

According to security expert Chris E. McGoey, 'the visible presence of a competent and confident bouncer will stop most trouble before it starts'. this is something that I wholeheartedly agree with. A large part of the role is being visible, not hiding away in the shadows in some dark corner of the pub or club.

It is helpful and expected Doorstaff to be dressed so they are recognizable as employees, although security-guard style uniforms are not appropriate for a Bouncer but smart attire in a uniform is a must, much respect can be gained from how you dress. Many people who cause trouble are reacting to the sense of an uncontrolled environment, and if they perceive from the moment they enter the club that things are under control, by seeing smart Bouncers who are standing out and who are alert trouble is less likely to start.

While physical confrontation is relatively rare, part of the role is being alert and being both prepared for it and confident in your actions. This confidence factor facing physical

Confrontation can often make it less likely to escalate. In order to do this role effectively you should be good judges of character, not easily insulted, easily intimidated and comfortable around other people.

But the biggest part of this is a sense of humor, useful in keeping the atmosphere relaxed and enjoyable for both customers and staff, to stop conflict before it gets out of hand and also to cope with some of the disturbing things that you will see and maybe even end up involved in during the course of your career.

Now a lot of what I have said above is all well and good in an ideal word but you will have occasions where when all other methods fail, it is sometimes necessary to eject unruly customers. Unlike the movies or on TV, this does not involve hurling them onto the path where they land in a puddle, or punching them in the face, this is where it's all about being calm and confident, not just in your own abilities but confident in your knowledge of the law. Violation of pub or nightclub rules is not always a crime, and bouncers have no legal right to manhandle a customer. If troublemakers refuse to leave when told to, they are then trespassing, and this is when you need to ensure that any use of physical force is both proportionate and reasonable.

Accurate record keeping is a must in this day and age more than anything else, records must be kept of all incidents, and how you record this can make or break any legal action or police prosecution that you may find yourself in, personally I always try and write my incident logs with as much detail as possible but you have to be meticulous on your paperwork, I have known some very good Bouncers that had trouble doing this, either because they were not good at describing things or they had issues with literacy or numerousy. These days both literacy and numerousy play a big part in the role so if this isn't your strong point, which it isn't for many, try and brush up on your skills before starting on the door, and never be afraid to ask for help.

Any Doorstaff will tell you that over the course of a career on the Door you will work all kinds of venues, from the stereotypical Nightclub or Pub, to sporting events and takeaways.

Once upon a time the humble domain of the Bouncer was kept to Pubs, Bars and Nightclubs but these days this is very different with more and more types of businesses recognizing the benefits of having good Doorstaff to reduce criminality of all kinds both in and around their business

Below you will find a bulleted list of the main tasks of the modern day Bouncer (Door Supervisor)

- Assist customer with any questions or concerns
- Have general knowledge of Health & Safety and Fire Policies and Procedures
- Monitor levels of Intoxication of customers
- Circulate throughout the venue, evaluating the conduct and attitudes of customers and looking for inappropriateness, Intoxication and misbehavior

- Monitor male-to-male behavior like fun fighting, arm wrestling etc. and possible early stages of altercations
- Interact and de-escalate verbal altercations between Patrons
- Maintain flow of foot traffic throughout the venue
- Lookout for hazards to customers and Staff, including: broken glass, bottles, chairs, tables, and any other possibly dangerous obstructions and ensure all fire exits are clear, unlocked and unobstructed at all times.
- Attend to the needs of over-intoxicated or physically ill customers
- Clear the venue on closing
- Report all Incidents and responses to Management and appropriate authorities
- Liaise and assist with any authority visit such as the Police, Fire Brigade, Local Council or the SIA
- Any Doorstaff will tell you that over the course of a career on the Door you will work all kinds of venues, from the stereotypical Nighlub or Pub, to sporting events and takeaways.

Chapter Eight

What makes a good Bouncer

Well that's the million dollar question if someone had the definitive answer on this then I would like them to prove it, first of all a common misconception is size, just because someone is 6ft 8" doesn't make them a good Doorman, but nor does it make them bad either. The most important thing in my mind a calm and steady demeanour, and authoritve voice and someone who is not easily scared, someone that won't back down.

Normally a good doorman can sense or even smell trouble a mile off and before it happens, there's no way of explaining this some people can and some people cant. I don't even think it's down to age, however experience in this game is a winner time and time again, I think its life experience. You also have to have the ability to calm situations verbally wherever you can, if you're really shy and are not capable of a bit of banter or quick thinking then this job is not for you.

One of the skills as mentioned is to have the ability to spot potential trouble before it happens and to be able to intervene, normally verbally to stop the trouble happening. If you can stop it before it starts you're laughing. A good Door Supervisor also needs honesty and integrity, you need to have the ability to put your personal feelings aside and treat everyone equally, regardless of Race, Religion, Gender or Sexuality.

The rules of the house apply to all, even your friends and family. You have house rules to enforce then they should be enforced fairly to everyone. An example that I once found myself in on a Door that I worked at was a ban on tracksuit bottom's it wasn't an upmarket venue so you can imagine it wasn't very popular but the house rules are the house rules, now I am at the door and I knock back someone for having tracksuit bottoms on, they start kicking off and eventually off they go, just then I see someone inside drinking with tracksuit bottoms on. This was a member of staff who had finished their shift in the kitchen and were having a drink after work. Yeah fair enough except they were right slap bang in front of the window for everyone to see with track suit bottoms on.

Now first of all, to all of the punters in the venue this looks like I am breaking the house rules that apply to everyone just because this one person was a staff member, many of them having been turned away in the past for wearing track suit bottoms. Secondly if the bloke who was kicking off at the front door had seen them it would again look as if I was showing favouritism to one person, or discriminating against him. After a conversation with the staff member who didn't seem to see anything wrong, I actually ejected them from the bar the same as I would with anyone else who had somehow managed to get in with track suit bottoms on. So you need to have integrity, be fair and most of all be consistent.

Now, you don't need to be Bruce Lee or Rocky Balboa to make a good Door Supervisor, remember you're not there to fight people when they get physical, you are there to stop the physical situation, to diffuse it and if anything to restrain and eject, but you do need to be fit, strong and for the want of a better phrase "Be able to handle yourself a bit".

I don't care what anyone says something a good Bouncer also needs is Bottle and Bottle in droves at times, anyone who has worked on a door for a period of time and says that they have never been worried or even scared in a situation is either a liar, a runner or a Physco and trust me you don't want any of these on your door.

Its fine to be scared at times when facing possible violent confrontation, in the of face fear this can sometimes be an advantage depending on how you control it. First of all never show it, if you show fear then straight away you have lost control of the situation, its really about keeping in check the body's natural 'Fight or Flight' instinct as in most Door situations you don't want to do either, you need to be somewhere in between.

Don't whatever you do go with the flight instinct and run away, if this is something that you do and you cannot control in conflict situations then your not going to be suited to this job, but equally you don't just want to go into 'Fight' and start throwing punches. You need to control and not show the fear and harness it to elude confidence and not fear, to be a figure of authority and not a figure of fun, and one of the most important things is, you must be willing to back up your team at all times and in any situation no matter what, you must be willing to die to protect your team.

To try and sum it up the best that I can the qualities to make a good Bouncer are these: (In no particular Order)

1. Honesty and Integrity

2. Authoritative

3. The ability to talk

4. The ability to not take things personally

5. The ability to control fear

6. Physically able to do the job

7. And to never, ever back down

8. Loyalty to your team

Chapter Nine

The SIA

For anyone who has been thinking of joining the ranks of the UK's Door Supervisors no doubt you will have heard a lot about the SIA or Security Industry Authority, but just who are the SIA and what do they do? The Security Industry Authority is the organisation responsible for regulating the private security industry. They are an independent body reporting to the Home Secretary, under the terms of the *Private Security Industry Act 2001*.

In government terms the SIA is there to:

"To regulate the private security industry effectively; to reduce criminality, raise standards and recognise quality service".

They have two main duties:

1. Licencing - Compulsory licensing of individuals undertaking designated activities within the private security industry

2. Approved Contractor Scheme - To manage the voluntary Approved Contractor Scheme, which measures private security suppliers against independently assessed criteria.

SIA licensing covers:

- Manned guarding
- Door supervision
- Close protection
- Cash and valuables in transit
- Public space surveillance using CCTV)
- Key holding
- Vehicle immobilising.

SIA licensing claims to ensure that private security operatives are *'fit and proper'* persons who are properly trained and qualified to do their job. The Approved Contractor Scheme introduced a set of operational and performance standards for suppliers of private security services. Those organisations that meet these standards are awarded Approved Contractor status.

Formed in 2003 under the terms of the Private Security Industry Act 2001as a 'Non-departmental public body' which is better known these days as a 'Quango'. Since its inception the SIA has always attracted heavy critisism from Industry, Government and people that work in the security industry. But like them or not at the current time if you wish to become a licensed Door Supervisor in the UK at present you MUST apply and be granted a license by the SIA.

If you work without an SIA license then the penalties are heavy **

Offence	Penalties
Engaging in licensable conduct without a licence [Section 3(1)] Contravening licence conditions [Section 9(4)] Obstructing SIA officials or those with delegated authority [Section 19(5)] False statements to the SIA [Section 22(1)]	Upon summary conviction at a Magistrates' Court or Sheriff Court., a maximum penalty of six months imprisonment and/or a fine of up to £5,000.
Employing unlicensed persons in licensable conduct [Section 5(1)] Using unlicensed vehicle immobilisers [Section 6(1)]	Upon summary conviction at a Magistrates' Court or Sheriff Court., a maximum penalty of six months imprisonment and/or a fine of up to £5,000. Upon conviction on indictment at Crown Court, High Court of Justiciary or Sheriff and jury trial, an unlimited fine and/or up to five years imprisonment.
Falsely claiming approved contractor status [Section 16 (2)] Providing private security services when not approved to do so [Section 17(2) & Section 17(3)]*	Upon summary conviction at a Magistrates' Court or Sheriff Court., a fine of up to £5,000. Upon conviction on indictment at Crown Court, High Court of Justiciary or Sheriff and jury trial, an unlimited fine.

Where an offence is committed by a body corporate and is committed with the consent or connivance of, or attributable to any neglect on the part of a director, manager, secretary or other similar officer of the body corporate, then that person is guilty of the offence and can be punished accordingly.

*An offence under section 17 of the Act can only be committed if it is made compulsory for private security companies to be approved under our Approved Contractor Scheme. The Act does allow for this, but there are no plans for that part of the Act to be brought into effect.

This is a simplification of the provision for offences and criminal penalties within the Private Security Industry Act 2001 (as amended).

A lot of people want to get into the business of becoming a Door Supervisor but don't even try as they have a criminal record, it is a phallasy that you will not be granted a license if you have a criminal record and the SIA state that each application is decided on its merits. Conflict based convictions are taken more seriously, as are those of firearms and the supply of illegal goods, however on the SIA website has a criminality checker which can give you guidance as to if top will be granted a license or not, this is however only guidance it doesn't guarantee a license will be granted.

http://www.sia.homeoffice.gov.uk/pages/licensing-cri.aspx

Chapter Ten

How do I become a bouncer

If you talk to any long term, door supervisor they will tell you that 'working the door' is under their skin. Before you consider becoming a door supervisor you should consider where you will be in 3 years' time when you approach your first SIA licence renewal. If you can see in advance that the job is not for you then why spend the money with the training, licence, various different uniforms in the first place?

A lot of people I speak to relating to training have the complete wrong attitude and think that spending 4 days in a classroom will turn them into the next great doorman. That approach needs to be seriously removed before anyone considers becoming a door supervisor. What you must realise is that the SIA door supervisor course is a level 2 qualification completed over 4 days training. This will prove that you're up to the required standard academically to be qualified in door supervision which will enable you to apply for your licence.

What is does not do is prepare you practically for working 'on the door' where you will potentially be dealing with drunk and/or drug fuelled people, taking verbal abuse, being threatened with someone's brother's mate's neighbour who just so happens to be the next world boxing champion. In my role as a tutor I also teach close protection courses which are run over a 14 consecutive day period and within that time frame I build in 3 mini-exercises and 1 big final exercise with a real live VIP, convoy of cars, shopping trips, theatre trips, restaurant visits etc. On the door supervisor course it's totally different, with the only confrontation you will be getting is the tutor carrying out some conflict management scenarios in the classroom under controlled conditions with no drink, drunks, weapons etc. It's a bit like when you pass your driving test and apply for your licence; we suddenly all think we are Lewis Hamilton, when in reality we are a million miles away from his level.

I advise you also ask yourself questions that will decide if you are suited to the job. Are you a people person? Can you communicate properly? Are you prepared to stand around for long hours with just your thoughts and imagination to keep you company? Can you handle the potential abuse that you will at some point have thrown at you? Do you think you will be able to handle conflict in a violent situation? There are numerous other questions you could ask yourself, however one of the most important questions I think you could ever ask yourself is one that you will never be able to answer until you are actually working which is how will you react, feel and deal with your first 'kick off' when working?

Unless you have been in a similar situation before then answering this question will purely be a false answer, and no classroom scenario will prepare you. Liken it to your favourite football team in pre-season training, they start off with an easy opponent where they probably win 5, 6, 7, 8 nil against a local team in the vicinity of their training camp. However when the first competitive match arrives on day one of the new season the pace of the game is very different, with a different opponent and their own tactics to win instead of rolling over as the local team did in pre-season. Now take that little comparison back into the world of a nightclub doorman and that is what your transition from classroom to front door will be like. During my younger days I used to train in boxing then latterly kick boxing and spent many years sparing in the gym. Boxing is a controlled art of fighting, in a gym when you are sober. Yes people get hurt in boxing, but all sparing is training. Boxing contests have a referee and medical facilities at first hand.

My son has trained for years in karate, competed in many tournaments and won many titles, all in a controlled environment. Put your mind into a violent situation, where drink and drugs can play a big factor in how the other person and/or group will react, there may be weapons such as knives, bottles, belt buckles involved which are not present in the ring or on a karate mat. Any medical facilities will be a first aider with a green box of bandages until a paramedic can get to you, and you will not have a referee to stop the fight before you get hurt. I have known the biggest, baddest, hardest gym and keep fit worshipers get a job on the door and as soon as they have been in their first violent situation they have either never returned to work or worse still they have hidden away and left their colleagues to deal with the trouble on their own.

So, you have decided that after a serious amount of soul searching you want to become a bouncer, or doorman, or door supervisor whatever you want to call yourself. One of the first things to take very important note of is that to become a successful door supervisor you do not have to be 6' 7", 22 stone and the heavyweight boxing champion of the world, neither do you have to be the local MMA champion or have a multitude of black belts. My own belief though that if you do some sort of fight training this will help you be prepared for when trouble comes your way, but it is not the be all and end all for becoming successful. Having the heart to do the job, the guts to not back down, the loyalty to work within a team and watch the back of your colleagues goes a very long way to making sure you will be valued at your job both by people you work for, you work with and yourself.

However, keeping yourself in a physically good condition will greatly help you when you have to get involved in situations in and around a licensed venue. The average fight lasts no more than 30 seconds, with anything lasting into minutes being considered a serious fight, with most fights getting split up and stopped within seconds. During the fight the number of punches thrown could range from 1 to anything up 15-20, even if it's a drunk throwing many punches and missing with most of them this will still be a physical fight.

Add more people to the fight and your physical exertion will be greatly heightened. Having been in numerous situations over the years, I am well aware that even in this short period of time I have been gasping for breath after a fight situation and that is with me still maintaining a reasonable level of fitness. But having said all this, being able to fight is not part of the SIA course and this is only guidance from myself as an active door supervisor.

I often get asked by women considering coming into the industry if the job is for them. Simple answer is yes. I strongly believe there are not enough girls coming through my training rooms, and you will find most doormen of today accept girls on the door with them. I know plenty of female door supervisors over the years who have done a better job than us men, and some of them have got more involved in dealing with trouble than the men on the team. In 1990 when I started out in the pubs and nightclubs of Colchester I can't recall having girls working on the door. The earliest I remember working with female door supervisors was around 1995 and then the club management and head doorman insisted they only search girls and check the toilets. In today's modern era there is very much a big role for women to play within the security industry, and as I mentioned just now, in my opinion there is just not enough girls working as door supervisors. During the late 90's I started working at a nightclub in Chelmsford and the two door girls who took turns to work at the club were literally employed to stand outside the toilet door and look pretty. If ever there was a fight within the club they were instructed not to get involved and to remain at the toilet. If any of us doormen noticed they were not standing outside the toilet then it was only as they themselves were in the toilet using it or they had gone to grab a drink from the bar.

Nowadays it is very different. In all my venues where I have been given the position of head doorman I have insisted on a female member of the team, and I invariably have them with me at the front door to search the girls, deal with situations involving girls, and also to be on hand to assist any other doorman within the whole club as opposed to just being stationed on a particular position and not move all night. Sometimes I have had the stupid comment made to me from management that having a door girl will just result in the doormen chatting them up and not doing the job; again a big mistake to think. Doormen will chat girls up as much as girls will chat doormen up.

It doesn't mean that because the two work together that it is an automatic green light for the door girl to be a target of sexual advances from her colleagues. Having said that I am well acquainted with the ways of the world and I am not naive enough to say that it wouldn't go on, but you would like to think all parties involved would remain professional while at work. In fact my long term partner is a licensed door supervisor and although we did not meet working in the same club, I have worked with her on numerous occasions since and we have always kept our private life and work life separate. We actually kept our whole relationship a secret for over a year so as not to allow prejudice against us from anyone should we of worked together.

We did have a funny event while working together when my partner had asked a young lad to leave a venue and as he stood protesting his case and getting nowhere, he then proceeded to offer her some advice with me standing there along the lines of "you need to go home and get your old man to give you one darling…. get rid of some of your frustration." This I found highly amusing and was trying extremely hard not to laugh at him, but this event leads onto another important factor of working on the door and that is to control your behaviour whilst working.

Becoming a 'Bouncer' in theory is easy; visit a training company, pay the course fees, complete the 4 days training, pass the exams, apply for the SIA licence, receive it and you are off and running. The reality is the hard bit. I won't beat around the bush, you will get abuse, whether it comes within your first week or not for a year… it will come. It's how you handle this abuse that will determine if you get a reputation as a good, professional worker. During the conflict management training I deliver I talk about the 4 A's – *manage the Abuse, don't get Angry, maintain a positive Attitude and be Assertive.*

I recently had an incident where I was informed by the venue manager that he suspected 2 lads of doing drugs in the toilet. I studied the CCTV monitor at the front door and sure enough a while later they both made their way into the toilet. I made my way upstairs and walked into the toilet where it was obvious one was in a cubicle and the other was acting sheepish outside. When I walked in the toilet the lad outside immediately started talking to me loudly and asked if I was called Ryder. I can't hide the fact that's my name and I am well known in Colchester so I simply replied with a yes, to which he then said he'd seen me on Bouncers, but as he said the word bouncers he said it louder and really made a point of over emphasising that word. It didn't need Einstein to work out that he was trying to communicate with his mate in the cubicle that I was outside. However the lad inside the cubicle clearly did not hear or more to the point as it turned out was a complete idiot, because he opened the door and walked straight out into me and looked startled that I was there. By this time the venue owner was with me and we both noticed that sitting on top of the toilet cistern was a big fat line of cocaine and a rolled up £5 note.

The owner brushed the cocaine into to the toilet and I asked both lads to finish their drinks as they took a brisk walk to the front door. This they did, still protesting their innocence and telling their two young female friends, who by this time had tagged along, that they had no idea why they were being thrown out. I'm not one for 'grassing' so I kept quiet and decided it's best for the lads to either come clean to the girls about their drug use or concoct some false story. All was going smoothly until the group were out on the street where all of a sudden, when the lads were out of my range, I started taking the usual abuse and threats. Picture the scene; me 42 years old, 6ft 1in, 20 stone, keeps reasonably fit with boxing and gym sessions standing there being told by an 18-19 year old, skinny 10 stone when wet dick head that I am about to be "Smashed Up". What did I do? Smile, politely inform him to go away and return another night to discuss it with me when he hasn't got traces of cocaine around his nose.

This is the concept of the four A's that you will need to adopt if you are going to forge a successful career as a door supervisor. Many people would ask why I didn't retaliate. My answer is to always look at the threat itself. I am well aware of the Law regarding self-defence and the use of force (I've been studying and teaching it since 2009) and knowing when and in what circumstances I can do something is key. In this instance the threat was verbal, the object of the threat was well outside my personal space and I had adopted my assertive body language to compliment my verbal communication with him thereby giving off the impression I did not want any trouble but at the same time I was prepared should he attempt something. Ok he was threatening to 'smash me up', but not from 10 foot away he can't.

Common Law within the UK allows us to defend ourselves if attacked, it does not allow for revenge or to teach someone a lesson, and if I had acted upon his words and very minor verbal threats then I could have found myself in trouble. Now, 20 years ago that young lad would have found himself asleep in the side street for the threats he was putting my way. That is not me sounding a bully as your mind probably still has the earlier image of myself aged 42 and the young lad aged 18-19, I am telling you straight as to how I would of dealt with that situation back then when I was 22 years old. There is no point me telling you in this book that I have been squeaky clean and never overstepped the mark, because you wouldn't believe me anyway.

Being able handle the abuse is one of the areas of being a door supervisor that you need to look at and ask yourself how you would react. Over the years, I and virtually every other door supervisor in the country has been threatened with some form of violence. At the top of the tree for combating this is the

Health & Safety at Work Act of 1974, where section 2 puts the responsibility on your employer to make your workplace safe for persons in their employment, and section 3 of the same Act imposes the same conditions for persons not in their employment. Section 2 covers you if you are PAYE and section 3 covers you if you are self-employed. If you are constantly subjected to workplace violence then it is down to the employer to rectify this by revaluing the risk assessment to make the workplace safe and therefore ease your stress levels at work, but do also consider that section 7 of the Act puts the onus on you the employee to look after your own health & safety while at work. So let's take it the venue has enough security staff and all avenues to reduce workplace violence and make you safe have been met so far as is reasonably practicable, and you still get the abuse. In what form will the abuse come? First of all we have the verbal abuse, and some of the regular favourites I have faced are; "fat cunt", "Wanker", "I shagged your Mum" and "I know where you live".

Physical abuse has been attacks on me while at work, being followed home and harassed while shopping in town with my then wife. Finally there is the criminal damage abuse where I have had my car keyed, windows smashed and tyres slashed. So how do we deal with these various forms of abuse and violence to ensure we remain within the Law and keep our SIA licence? That is down to one person only - you. I can tell you in my training everything you need to know regarding the Law and how to operate, or I can type it in this book and you read what is right and wrong, then later down the line you turn up for work on the door having had a bad day, perhaps an argument with your partner, you are running late for work and you arrive with an off attitude.

Then when you are working and trying to not let your attitude effect your work, you encounter the situation I described earlier with the cocaine use and the threats of being smashed up by some dick head who is brave as fuck when 10 feet away. You 'lose it' and act upon his small and inconsiderate threat by launching as assault on him and you get into trouble. Even if in this one off situation you did not get arrested, your actions could have a negative effect on you in terms of employment at the venue or with the security company you work for, it could cause retribution against you, the venue or the company from any family or friends of the young lad, which turns full circle to my question at the top of this chapter… *'where you will be in 3 years' time when you approach your first SIA licence renewal'*? If you do not act in a professional and appropriate way you may not even get to that first 3 yearly renewal.

Chapter Eleven

Training

Having been an SIA tutor since 2009 the first thing I want to say to anyone wishing to attend any security training course... actually no the first thing I want to *shout* to anyone wishing to attend any security training course is **READ THE BLOODY JOINING INSTRUCTIONS!** So many students turn up in class without the correct identification, or the correct clothing for physical intervention training or correct learning tools with them. Any reputable company will send you joining instructions to inform you of what is required of you for the course. The most important thing for you to be aware of is the identification that you need to bring with you to confirm you are who you say you are. Without it then the training company cannot train you, even if you have paid up front for your course. An inspector from the SIA or the awarding body can turn up at any time to do an audit of the course and if the tutor, invigilator or company have allowed you to train and take exams without the required ID then they will be in trouble. So what *should* be in the joining instructions? Below is a list some of the basic things you should be informed of and I shall talk about each one in turn;

Start and finish date

You will need to know when your course starts and finishes. Almost all training companies offer differing training days. Some run from a Monday to Thursday, some run midweek into the weekend, some run over two weekends; either way the course *must* run over a minimum of 4 days. There is nothing wrong with a training company running their courses longer than the 4 days should they be offering you additional 'bolt-on' courses or modules within their course, but the SIA side of the training must be no less than 4 days. Any 'bolt-on' modules or courses built in are over and above the SIA requirement and therefore do not make up part of the course structure.

Start and finish times each day

You must obviously know when your course starts and finishes each day. There are very strict guidelines for all training companies to follow as set by the SIA itself and these are called Guided Learning Hours (GLH) and Guided Contact Hours (GCH). The current requirements for the door supervisor course are 38 GLH of which a minimum of 30 must be contact time, and that no more than 8 hours a day can be spent in the classroom. An extract from the door supervision course specification from my awarding body Highfield Awarding Body of Compliance[1] states;

> *"The SIA has stated that the training, delivery and assessment of the Level 2 Award in Door Supervision (QCF) must take place over a minimum of four days. Because of this, centres will no longer be permitted to conduct training courses and assessments for this qualification in less than the mandatory training period of four days. Each day of training must not exceed eight hours. This requirement applies to all SIA Approved Awarding Organisations offering the Level 2 Door Supervision qualification (QCF), and*

---

[1] Highfield Body of Compliance (HABC) are one of 9 awarding bodies in the UK approved to offer the qualifications required to apply for the SIA licence.

they will be monitoring training providers to ensure compliance. This requirement was introduced on 1 December 2012."

Location of venue

The joining instructions will inform you of where your course will be taking place, with some instructions giving you a room location if the company knows it, i.e. a room hired within a college or hotel. If the joining instructions do not list any parking facilities or public transport arrangements then this is an area that I advise you to research before your course. Don't leave everything to the last minute and arrive late on day one of the course. Not only do you have to comply with the GCH, a lot of us tutors are either contacted by the security companies you may end up applying for jobs with, or we recommend people to companies. If you are late and blame it on parking, traffic, bus or train was late then these are the sort of things a potential employer would want to know. If you cannot get to a training course on time then who's to say you will get to your shift on the door on time?

List of required ID

As I have mentioned earlier, you must bring the required ID as set by the SIA in order to sit the exams, this is down to you to ensure you have this before you attend the course. You must bring original documents and not photocopies, and I advise you have them and bring them on day one of your course. Although the guidelines I follow as set down by HABC state the invigilator must check the ID before the examinations take place, I personally like to check first thing on day one to ensure that the student has the correct ID in the first place. I could quite happily adopt a 'take the money and run' attitude, but I prefer to take ownership of the students and ensure they have the correct ID, and if not I can advise them what they must additionally bring before they sit their exams. For a list of ID required it is best to check first with the training company if it is not listed on the joining instructions or is not clear enough then check the SIA's website where the current list will be available for you to read.

Up to date passport sized photograph

You must bring a passport sized photograph that resembles you in your current form. Quite simply go and get some taken a few days before your attend the course, however if you have some recently taken photos to hand that still depict you are you are now then they will be fine. Obviously if you have some photos that may have been taken a few months earlier you may have a change of hair style, or facial hair in the case of males, but providing this does not substantially change your whole appearance then they will be fine. Note I worded it as a 'passport sized photograph', this is due to an unbelievable incident I once had in the training room. Whilst checking the ID and photographs of a class I told a lad who had not got a photograph that he must bring me a passport photo the next day. The following day he brought me his passport photo and I looked at it and for a second or two and thought it didn't look and feel like every other photo I had encountered. It was only after these initial first few seconds that I then noticed it was heavily laminated and stiff. I then questioned the student as to where he got the photo from, and his reply to this day still amuses me; "you asked for a passport photo so I cut it out of my passport." From that day on I have always worded and asked for a passport sized photo for this reason and I recite with amusement this story, however I am aware to a point he was only complying with my instructions. I have also had students bring in a passport sized photo of them 20 years younger. No good, it must be an up to date photo.

<u>What material you may be required to bring</u>

Included within your course fees should be all the materials you need to complete the course. However some training companies may not provide everything you individually require. Pens, pencils, rubber, paper and perhaps a course book should be provided. However it is probably best to take along a pen, pencil and a notepad and do enquire if a course book is provided. The training PowerPoint I use is complimented with a course book and this is provided free of charge on day one, and I would question any training provider that makes you pay for the course book as an additional extra. Of course you do indirectly pay for this course book as the cost of it really should be built into the course cost. I must point out that it is not a requirement for the training provider to provide any course book. Some companies may offer you a digital course book which you can access from any laptop, PC, tablet or smart phone. If they do be aware they may have the facility built in whereby they can monitor every time you log in and read the book. This will especially be important if you are required to do any prior learning before attending such as on the Upskilling course or any course where additional learning is a requirement.

<u>Clothing</u>

There is no set clothing requirements for modules 1-3 of the door supervisor course. As a general rule suitable classroom clothing will be acceptable, however each training provider may have their own requirements. I personally allow shorts in the summer however I do know training companies and/or even individual tutors that ask for a smarter appearance. For module 4 which is the physical intervention day then suitable gym gear should be worn. I have in the past been questioned when I emphasise to the students that for the PI module they must have trainers, tracksuit and an old T shirt. People have quite rightly said that when working on the door we don't wear gym gear, but more so a shirt, tie, trousers and shoes; however when you are in a training environment you need to dress accordingly. We tutors have to either have our own insurance in place for instructing this module, or the company will hold the insurance. Part of the conditions to this insurance will more than likely state that the participants must be dressed accordingly. If you regularly attend a gym for keep fit or body building purposes then I am sure you would not attempt to train in a suit, tie and shoes; so why do it in a training environment here? If you have an accident whereby you have slipped over in shoes and injure yourself, the tutor or training company could be held liable so therefore any good training company who is looking after your health on this module will insist you are dressed accordingly.

In addition to all of these you could have additional extra items that the individual training company may add. Some of the ones I have seen included company policies relating to drink and drug use, which awarding body the course is certificated by and appeals procedure. Please note this list is not exhaustive and not a must for every training company to list on their joining instructions.

Before you get into the classroom and if your first language is not English, the SIA, in consultation with Skills for Security, have specified the following:

"Communication in English is an integral requirement of the SIA competencies. This is made explicit in particular competence statements and in relation to the title of the part, or lesson, which deals with 'Communication and Conflict Management'. Learners also need to demonstrate their competence in English in an applied context in relation to other areas of the specifications and competence needs to be considered holistically, with the aim that the learner should be able to demonstrate these same competencies effectively in the workplace. To not be able to do so could have health and safety implications for the individual, and for others, in the workplace. For the above reasons, it would not be appropriate for learners for whom English is their second language to be provided with a scribe or reader to assist them in their assessment. To do so would also provide an unfair advantage to such learners. Centres should be advised to carry out an initial assessment of learners to identify their particular needs at the earliest stage. In the case of learners for whom English language communication skills are a weakness (and other particular needs considerations do not apply) it would be appropriate to direct them to undertake additional learning to develop these skills."

So taking the above statement into account, training companies should have systems in place to test learnings who fall into this category. It is recommended that learners whose first language is not English must complete a level 1 literacy test prior to starting on the course. When this is done and how is down to the individual training company, with most I have worked with opting to offer an initial assessment at the training centre at the time of booking the course. This however doesn't work if the company are offering online bookings or telephone bookings, so a procedure where the literacy test is carried out first thing in the training room should be fitted into the first day's schedule.

When you get to the classroom on the first day and depending on who you train with and which awarding body they are with then you may spend best part of the first hour doing paperwork, having your ID checked, running through course procedures and requirements. A good tutor will run through the Health & Safety aspects of the training environment before they do anything just in case a fire alarm goes off or you need the toilet etc. I always introduce myself before I complete any paperwork, and I carry out an ice-breaker with the students. This can be a basic introduction to each other, or pair the students up and get them to introduce their partner having asked questions, or a speed dating style introduction where all the students and tutor engage in a 30 second each quick fire introduction before moving on until everyone has met each other, or a game such as a true and false game whereby you have to inform the class of 2 true and 1 false story about yourself and the others have to pick which is the lie. When I introduce myself I keep it basic and to the point, I talk briefly about my career as a door supervisor including where I have worked and which venues I have been head doorman at, I mention my introduction into close protection work and then I talk about when I started tutoring and why. I like to explain why I got into tutoring because I like the students to see me as a man who is giving back to the industry all his experience to ensure his students have the best training he can offer. My own opinion is that good training comes from experience of doing the job first hand and not from a tutor who decides to gain their teaching qualifications and stand up in front of a class and recite from a PowerPoint presentation. I personally will not teach any subject I know nothing about or have not carried out my own training and CPD in beforehand. For instance I can teach anyone how to be a door supervisor all day long, but I would never attempt to teach someone how to dismantle and put back together an engine.

So once you have completed all the paperwork, ID checks, introductions, health & safety briefing then you will start to get down to the main reason of being on the course... learning the basics on how to be qualified as a door supervisor. I shall now run you through the 4 individual modules (sometimes called units) of the course outlining what the aims and objectives of each module which will outline what you will be taught. Before you read through these aims and objectives I want to point out that I have taught for numerous training companies in my position as a self-employed trainer and different companies have different methods of working and they use different awarding bodies. Also us tutors use different methods of tutoring and have our own preferred PowerPoint packages to deliver the training from. I personally use the training materials from Highfield Ltd[2] as they are also a sister company of the main awarding body I use, however everyone – company and tutors alike – must comply with the learning outcomes as listed on the next few pages.

_____

Chapter Twelve

Learning Moduales

Module 1: Working in the Private Security Industry

Lesson 1
Aim: know the purpose and main features of the private security industry.

Learning Outcomes:
- Define the main purposes of the private security industry
- Identify different sectors and career opportunities within the private security industry
- State the main aims of the Private Security Industry Act
- Identify the main functions of the Security Industry Authority and other key bodies within the private security industry
- Describe the main qualities required by security industry operatives

Lesson 2

Aim: understand the legislation that is relevant to people working in the private security industry.

Learning Outcomes:
- Identify the differences between civil and criminal law
- Identify aspects of human rights legislation that are relevant to the private security industry
- State the data protection principles outlined in data protection legislation
- Describe types of discrimination that can occur in the workplace
- Identify how equal opportunities legislation applies in the workplace

Lesson 3

Aim: understand relevant aspects of health and safety in the workplace.

Learning Outcomes:
- Outline the importance of health and safety in the workplace
- Identify the main responsibilities of employees, employers and the self-employed under health and safety legislation
- Identify ways of minimising risk to personal safety and security
- Identify typical hazards in the workplace
- Describe safe methods of manual handling
- Identify commonly used safety signs
- Describe appropriate reporting procedures for accidents and injuries

Lesson 4

Aim: Know how to apply the principles of fire safety.

Learning Outcomes:
- Identify the three components that must be present for fire to exist
- Describe how fire can be prevented
- Identify fires by their classification
- Identify the types and uses of fire extinguishers and firefighting equipment
- State appropriate responses on discovering a fire
- Explain the importance of understanding fire evacuation procedures

Lesson 5
Aim: know how to deal with non-fire-related workplace emergencies

Learning Outcomes:
- Define the term 'emergency' when used in the workplace
- Identify types of workplace emergencies
- Identify appropriate responses to workplace emergencies
- Outline the procedures for dealing with bomb threat warning calls
- Identify appropriate responses to situations requiring first aid

Lesson 6
Aim: understand the principles of effective communication and customer care in the private security industry.

Learning Outcomes:
- Describe the elements of the communication process
- Identify methods of verbal and non-verbal communication

- Identify common barriers to communication
- State the importance of effective communication in the workplace
- Identify different types of customers and how their needs can vary
- Describe the principles of customer care

Module 2: Working as a Door Supervisor

Lesson 1
Aim: understand the behaviour appropriate for individual door supervisors, as defined by the SIA's 'Standards of Behaviour'.

Learning Outcomes:
- Identify the key elements of the SIA's Standards of Behaviour for door supervisors
- State the reasons why standards of behaviour are required
- Identify the requirements specifically relating to SIA licensing
- Define the role and objectives of the door supervisor
- Identify the key qualities of a door supervisor

Lesson 2
Aim: understand the elements of civil and criminal law relevant to door supervisors.

Learning Outcomes:
- State the law relating to use of force
- Identify the different types of assault as defined by law
- List offences against property that a door supervisor may come across
- State the options available to a door supervisor when the law is broken

Lesson 3
Aim: understand search procedures and the reasons for having them.

Learning Outcomes:

- State the importance of an admissions policy
- Identify common areas that can be included in an admissions policy
- Identify the reasons for searching premises
- State how to search people and their property
- State the differences between general, random and specific searches
- Identify the hazards involved with conducting searches and appropriate precautions that can be taken
- State the definitions of offensive weapons
- Outline the procedures for handling and recording articles, including drugs, seized during a search

Lesson 4
Aim: understand the powers of arrest and related procedures

Learning Outcomes:
- Identify indictable offences
- Identify factors to consider when deciding whether to make a citizen's arrest
- Outline the procedures for making a citizen's arrest
- Outline the procedures to be followed after a citizen's arrest

Lesson 5
Aims: understand relevant drug legislation and its relevance to the role of the door supervisor.

Learning Outcomes:
- Identify aspects of current drugs legislation that apply to the role of the door supervisor
- State the common indicators of drug misuse
- Identify common types of illegal drugs
- State how to recognise signs of drug dealing

- Outline the procedure for dealing with customers found to be in possession of drugs
- State how to dispose of drug related litter and waste safely

Lesson 6
Aim: understand incident recording and crime scene preservation.

Learning Outcomes:
- Identify the types of, and reasons for, records needed to be kept by a door supervisor
- Identify incidents which need to be recorded and when the police are to be called
- State the procedures for record keeping
- Identify the different types of evidence
- Outline the rules to be followed to appropriately preserve evidence and crime scenes

Lesson 7
Aim: understand licensing law and social responsibility

Learning Outcomes:
- State the licensing objectives under current alcohol licensing legislation
- State the different types of licences issued and the activities they allow
- State circumstances under which customers can be ejected
- State police powers with regard to licensed premises
- State the powers of entry of authorised persons
- Outline the rights and duties of licensees and door supervisors as their representatives
- Outline relevant legislation regarding children and young people

- Identify activities considered unlawful under licensing, gaming and sexual offences legislation

Lesson 8
Aim: understand and be able to follow procedures for emergency situations.

Learning Outcomes:
- Identify common human responses in an emergency situation
- State the reasons for having fire risk assessments and maximum occupancy figures
- Identify behaviours that could indicate unusual and suspicious activity
- Identify current counter terrorism issues and procedures as they relate to the role of a door supervisor
- Identify common situations requiring first aid that occur in licensed premises
- State how to safely dispose of contaminated waste

Module 3: Conflict Management

Lesson 1
Aim: understand the principles of conflict management appropriate to their role.

Learning Outcomes:
- State the importance of positive and constructive communication to avoid conflict
- Identify the importance of employer policies, guidance and procedures relating to workplace violence
- Identify factors that can trigger an angry response in others
- Identify factors that can inhibit an angry response in others
- Identify how managing customer expectations can reduce the risk of conflict
- Identify human responses to emotional and threatening situations

Lesson 2
Aim: understand how to recognise, assess and reduce risk in conflict situations.

Learning Outcomes:
- Identify the stages of escalation in conflict situations
- Explain how to apply dynamic risk assessment to a conflict situation

Lesson 3
Aim: understand how to communicate effectively in emotive situations and deescalate conflict.

Learning Outcomes:

- State how to use non-verbal communication in emotive situations
- Identify how to overcome communication barriers
- Identify the differences between assertiveness and aggression
- Identify ways of defusing emotive conflict situations
- Identify appropriate approaches to take when confronting unacceptable behaviour
- Identify how to work with colleagues to deescalate conflict situations
- State the importance of positioning and exit routes

Lesson 4
Aim: understand how to develop and use problem solving strategies for resolving conflict.

Learning Outcomes:
- State the importance of viewing the situation from the customer's perspective
- Identify strategies for solving problems
- Identify win-win approaches to conflict situations

Lesson 5
Aim: understand good practice to follow after conflict situations.

Learning Outcomes:
- State the importance of accessing help and support following an incident
- State the importance of reflecting on and learning from conflict situations
- Identify the importance of sharing good practice
- State the importance of contributing to solutions to re-occurring problems

Module 4: Physical Intervention Skills for the Private Security Industry

Lesson 1
Aim: understand physical interventions and the legal and professional implications of their use.

Learning Outcomes:
- Identify the differences between defensive physical skills and physical interventions
- Identify the differences between non-restrictive and restrictive interventions
- Identify positive alternatives to physical intervention
- State the importance of only using physical intervention skills as a last resort
- State legal implications relating to the use of physical interventions

Lesson 2
Aim: understand how to reduce the risk of harm when physical intervention skills are used.

Learning Outcomes:
- State the importance of dynamic risk assessment in situations where physical intervention skills are used
- Identify the risk factors involved with the use of physical interventions
- Identify ways of reducing the risk of harm during physical interventions
- State responsibilities immediately following physical interventions
- State the importance of keeping physical intervention knowledge and skills current

Lesson 3

Aim: be able to use non-pain related physical skills to protect yourself and others from assault.

Learning Outcomes:
- Demonstrate non-aggressive stance and positioning skills
- Demonstrate non-aggressive skills used to evade and protect against blows
- Demonstrate non-aggressive methods of disengagement from grabs and holds
- Demonstrate non-aggressive methods to stop one person assaulting another
- Demonstrate non-aggressive team methods to separate persons fighting
- Communicate professionally with the subject of physical intervention, colleagues and other customers while protecting yourself and others from assault

Lesson 4

Aim: be able to use non-pain related standing holding and escorting techniques, including non-restrictive and restrictive skills.

Learning Outcomes:
- Demonstrate the use of a method for physically prompting a person
- Demonstrate the use of a non-restrictive method of escorting a person
- Demonstrate the use of a one-person low level restrictive standing hold that can be used as an escort
- Demonstrate the use of a two-person restrictive standing hold that can be used as an escort
- Demonstrate how to provide support to colleagues during a physical intervention

- Demonstrate how to de-escalate and disengage a physical intervention ensuring safety for both parties
- Communicate professionally with the subject of physical intervention, other customers and colleagues, while using prompting, holding and escorting techniques

Lesson 5
Aim: understand good practice to follow after physical interventions.

Learning Outcomes:
- State the importance of accessing help and support following an incident
- State the importance of reflecting on and learning from physical intervention situations
- Identify additional factors when reporting and accounting for use of force

As of 1 November 2013 all training companies must deliver a new mandatory unit centred on vulnerable people. The SIA have stipulated that the following areas of additional training must be delivered by all centres;

- Identifying Vulnerable People
- Understanding the risks to vulnerable people being ejected from, or refused entry to, a venue, and what actions can be taken to protect them
- Identifying the Behaviour of Sexual Predators
- Identifying indicators of Child Sexual Exploitation

These new requirements have arisen out of work that the SIA has completed with the Home Office and Northumbria Police following an incident that occurred in Newcastle with a 17 year old girl, details of which I will not go into here. I am all for this new unit having worked in the mid 90's at a nightclub in Guildford where in 1999 a young girl was ejected by the door staff for appearing to be drunk and was refused re-entry to wait for her friends. Later that evening she was attacked and murdered in a flat where she had been lured to by an older man. Now although I was not working there by then, and although the door staff did not commit the murder, I still always used to mention this incident during my training prior to this new mandatory unit being introduced to highlight that although the laws of the UK state people must not remain on a licensed premises when drunk, at the same time we must consider their safety and wellbeing.

It is the responsibility of all training companies and tutors to comply with these learning outcomes and therefore you as the student must be taught all of the above criteria in order to pass your multiple choice exam. The powerpoints I use 'blend' a lot of the learning outcomes together and I go through the PowerPoint presentation from start to finish, but I elaborate on the slides with knowledge and experience to enhance the learning experience. I don't claim to be the best tutor in the country, in fact I am always looking at ways to improve my own tutoring skills, but what I can pride myself on is having worked 'on the door' since early 1990 then I can bring that experience into the training room to give my students a good insight into what it will be like when they get into work.

At this point I would like to add an opinion I personally have of the training as it is at the moment. There has been a consultation with the SIA for updated qualification specifications across all areas of SIA qualification, however I have my own views on the level of training. I strongly believe that the 4 days training in a classroom is not enough to ready people for what they are going to face out there on the streets. Okay, when I started in 1990 I had no training, no licence and no idea of what I was walking into. I had about 3-4 days' notice that I was working the following Saturday night and the most I had to do was go and buy a white shirt and a bow tie. When I teach close protection students I have them for 138 hours over a period ranging between 12 and 14 days and during this period I take the students out and about around London and the surrounding areas on 'mini exercises' and then we spend the final 2 days solid on the 'final exercise'. During these exercises the students are out on the ground working with myself and whoever I call in as our VIP in the role of a close protection operative. I try to get as much realism as I can into the close protection course.

Going back to the 4 day door supervisor course and my reasons why I think it is not long enough. When you get to work on the door as a door supervisor you can go weeks without facing any trouble whatsoever and then bang... 2, 3, 4 fights in a night, the adrenaline will be rushing through your body, your fear will be rising up and down at a constant rate, you could be threatened, or spat at, or punched, or kicked, or god forbid seriously hurt. Then the following night when the time gets close to leaving home and going to work that's the time you realise if you are cut out to be a door supervisor.

I think the course should be the 3 days theory in the classroom whereby you learn the foundations required to start work. The physical intervention should be extended to a 2 days with more spent on self-defence for you the door supervisor facing the violence. Then you take and have to pass the exams as normal to get your licence, however this is a provisional licence like you get before you can drive a car on the road on your own. This provisional licence is then your authority to work aided on the door in a team of experienced door supervisors or for an established company where you are assessed a bit similar to an NVQ. I think you should always work with people, and they report back to your assessor over a period such as 3 months or a minimum amount of completed hours. Then when you have passed this probationary period with your provisional licence you gain a full pass and the SIA grant you a full licence where you can work full time unaided as a door supervisor.

But, as it stands that is my own personal belief and I must point out it is not the view of the SIA, any awarding body or anyone else connected with this book.

Chapter Thirteen

Choosing the Right Training

Choosing the right training can be a difficult decision because of the vast number of providers offering SIA training. I advise anyone looking for a training course is not to just head for the cheapest option because the 'saying you pay for what you get' can sometimes be very true in this case, but it also may not apply in certain cases. Some training companies I work for charge as low as £140 for a 4 day course whereas others charge in excess of £200 sometimes close to £250 for the same course. What you need to be aware of is the learning outcomes as produced and set by the SIA are the same whether you pay £140 or £250, the guided learning hours are the same and the requirements for the examination and the physical intervention assessment is exactly the same.

There will be a slight difference in the number of questions per exam, the amount of time you get to complete the exam and the physical intervention training system that you will be taught, but at the end of the day whatever price you pay, however many questions you get asked in your written test, whatever physical intervention system you learn and whatever awarding body eventually issue you a certificate you will still get the exact same SIA licence as the next person and at the same cost of £220. Now without sounding big headed I feel I offer a high end quality door supervisor course not just because I have been on national TV and people know my face, but because I can stand there and tell you things that have happened and are a true account of what the job is about. We can all sit down in a classroom and learn in a nice warm cosy environment where you have a text book to back up what the tutor and powerpoints are telling you, but what the text book or powerpoints don't tell you is what it will really be like standing in the freezing cold, bored out your brains, trying to stay focused having been awake 15, 16, 17 or even 18 hours…. and then World War 3 kicks off and you have to deal with it.

But I can tell you what it's like as I have been there. Of course I am not the only trainer in the country in this situation, and I never have or will lay claim to being the best trainer in the country, but what I will stand by is that with over 24 years' service on the door I can give you a better course than a tutor who just has their teacher qualifications and have done very limited door supervision work. So I suggest your first question to any prospective training provider is to ask who the tutor will be and what their background is.

If you are of the mind-set that you will pay the lowest fee possible just to get that same licence as the next person who perhaps paid £100 more than you, then you are perhaps barking up the wrong tree. As I mentioned just now about pricing, you may not always get a lesser tutor on the cheaper course for example as I said I teach for a company that charge £140 so those students are getting a good course for a really good price, whereas the following week I could be teaching at another training provider where they charge £250 but the course is the same and the students will be getting the same input from me. I still get my day rate of pay no matter what the students pay so it does not bother me one way or another. You must however weigh up the overall costs before diving straight in and getting the course for the cheapest option. I have had hundreds of emails, Facebook and Twitter messages from people asking to train with me since I was on Bouncers, and most of the companies I teach for would let me do a deal for anyone booking through me, however I teach mainly in the London area so in order to perhaps save £30, £40, £50 off a course booked through me you would have to probably spend double that on weekly travel into or around London. Same theory applies when you are looking for the cost of the course; book a course at £140 and have to travel resulting in high travel costs as opposed to booking a higher priced course but closer to home therefore saving the travel. I am honoured that people want to train with me and if they still want to travel down to London then I will happily train anyone but do watch the cost and remember I do not claim to be the best tutor.

The company or training provider you eventually choose should also be a big deciding factor on your decision to go with them because as I have just said the learning outcomes required for you to achieve are all the same. If a training provider skips any or does not complete the required contact hours of tuition then ultimately the SIA could, and more than likely will suspend your licence until you complete the training. This will technically not be your fault as you would have only taken direction from the training provider however you would have not met the required standard of learning to gain the qualification even though you may have taken and passed the examinations with no problem at all. My advice is to research the training provider by any means possible such as internet forums or Facebook comments, but don't just read any negative stuff about them, do look for the good comments and make your own judgement. I once had a student complain about me and my style of tutoring to the point where he said I did not know what I was on about when I gave the lesson on The Use of Force and the different avenues of UK Law where you can self-defend yourself, use the pre-emptive strike and your right to defend your life under Article 2 of The Human Rights Act 1998, his point being that he disagreed with me when I said you can hit first rather than wait to be hit. One thing you will never find fault with me on is the Law as I have studied it for years under the exceptional guidance of Mark Dawes from The National Federation for Personal Safety, however that topic is not for discussion here. This student argued with me in class, refused to except what I was saying with regards to what you can and cannot do both in terms of legality on the pre-emptive strike and also on virtually every true account of experience I happened to discuss in class to the point where I was very close to removing him as he was becoming a distraction to the other students. Ultimately this student failed his exams, all three of them and miserably too whereas all other 7 or 8 students in the class passed with very high marks. The upshot of this is the student complained about me and if you were to read his complaint should it of been on an internet forum then you would of probably taken the decision of not to train with me or the company I was teaching for as he really went to town. None of the other students complained and everyone on that particular course gave me nothing but high praise, and to date this complaint is one of only two that have ever been put in against me. When I last calculated my pass rate around 88% of my students pass their whole course first time with virtually everyone passing upon a resit of their exam. I have and would read any complaint against me seriously but in this instance I have no reason to worry that I may be 'struck off' all the companies I train for. So do read as many reviews as necessary before you decide which company you are going to give your money to and don't just read one person's account of their experience as it may be a malicious jibe towards the tutor or company.

The next thing I would look at is the training venue and ask yourself how accessible it is to you with regards to travel. How long will it take? Is it easily accessible with public transport? Is there parking and if so is there a charge? All this will mount up and add to the overall cost that you will be paying out of your pocket to get that licence. Also consider the facilities at the venue you are going to be visiting such as drink facilities or air conditioning because after all you are going to be sitting in a training room for up to 8 hours a day, it becomes very tiring and you really want to be learning in the best environment. Not every training room *must* have air conditioning but that's just a pointer I personally feel is important as a tutor. If you can open a window that's fine, but from my own perspective I know if I was sitting on the other side of the fence and myself being on a course in a hot stuffy room with no ventilation or air conditioning then I would not be learning in an effective way. The venue is an important factor in for you to consider but let's face facts you are only on a 4 day course, it's not like you are there for months so I would not make yourself look like a diva and demand everything be like a 5 star hotel.

Chapter 14

Tests

Everyone hates an exam. I do, but I also embrace them as without them we don't get the qualification that we need so I give myself the mind-set that I will pass. I advise you all to have the same train of thought...... that you will pass and failure is not an option. Let me tell you a story; my youngest son Tyler went for a grading for his next karate belt, he is one of those sporty kids that is good at whatever he does even to the point of supporting the magnificent Southampton FC just like his Dad! He had only failed one grading to date but wasn't confident on this grading because he could not do some kick where he had to spin round, jump up and kick to the head. He tried and tried and tried this kick for weeks and could not get it right at all, and if I recall he would probably do 1 good one for 4 bad ones and therefore started to tell himself he could not do it.

This became the norm for the weeks leading up to the grading date, but he still went in for the grading along with all the other kids. As he came out from behind the curtain I saw his face and immediately knew he had failed, then Sean the Sensei came out and he caught my eye and I could see from his face he was about to fail Tyler. On the way home I spoke to Tyler and he said it was the worst grading he had ever done because he was that worried about the kick that he forgot his katas and just generally messed it all up. I told him not to worry and he can re-grade in 6 weeks' time, and that I will help him to which he gave me a funny look as I have as much knowledge of karate training as I do flying a jet fighter...

none. However all I did over the forthcoming weeks up to the re-grading was to tell Tyler that he could do the kick and that he was doing well despite the fact that he still could not do the kick perfectly. I continued to install this positive train of thought into Tyler and slowly over the weeks he started to forget the "I cannot do it" approach so that on his grading he flew through and passed to gain his next belt. The truth is he could not do the kick any better on the re-grading than that what he could when he failed the grading 6 weeks earlier, but going into the grading with the positive thought that he *could* do it enabled him not to worry about it and when it came to doing the kick for the grading panel he did it perfectly. That is a little insight into how powerful the brain is and how negative thoughts can affect you and result in you maybe failing your exams based on you creating a little world that you cannot get out of because you think negative all the time.

Believe it or not the brain cannot process a negative for example; fill a glass full of juice and give it to a young toddler and ask them to take it over to the table they will 9 times out of 10 do it without any problems, but you install a negative into their brain first by telling them "do not spill it"; what will they do? They will spill it because that is what they are then thinking about. You think about failing your exams then you will fail them before you even get into the training room, as I did my HGV driving test many years ago because I convinced myself I would fail it.

The exams are not hard, they are multiple choice answers A, B, C or D whereby you chose one of them as your correct answer. You can change your mind on the answer you have given as many times as you like until either you hand the answer sheet in or you run out of time, but remember there is only one correct answer per question and not a choice of 2. So many students tell me after that on some questions they could not make their mind up as there was a possible 2 answers they could have given so therefore they just picked one. If you are not sure on the answer perhaps leave it and move on, then come back to the question later.

There appears to be no set number of questions allowed to be asked as each awarding body I have taught under have a different number of questions per exam module, but the concept remains the same in that there is only one correct answer. There is also no actual writing answers down on your part, you just select the answer you think and indicate on the answer sheet your choice A, B, C or D, however I do admit that on some of the answers given there could be a justifiable reasoning for a couple of them to be correct but unfortunately the exams are not a verbal discussion and you must select one answer only. You will be given a time frame to complete each individual exam in and this will strictly be followed by the invigilator taking charge of the exam, but again each awarding body I have taught for seem to have slightly differing times to complete. Your invigilator should give you adequate prior notice of the exam start and finish times, and also give you a count down near the end. If I am called into invigilate for another tutor I normally give the students a countdown from half way in to the end ensuring that towards the end I increase the countdown. I normally inform them when they have 15 minutes left, then 5 minutes, then 2 minutes and finally time up to which at this point all exams must stop.

During your exams you must not talk to anyone in the room, you are not allowed to use a mobile phone or any other device with internet capability except the tablet device your exam maybe carried out on as HABC are soon to be pioneering online exams, you must not leave the room except in an emergency evacuation (for which you will receive extra time onto your exam should this be the case), you are not allowed to have any notes or reference books with you (HABC allow an English dictionary), you must not ask the invigilator for any advice on any question as the SIA require everyone to have a good understanding of English and you cannot change any answers after you hand in the exam. Many times I have had students finish and leave the exam room at the end and when they chat with each other outside they all discuss their questions and suddenly someone realises they have a question wrong and wants to change their answer. This cannot be done and based on that this is why I advise you all to utilise the time you are given and check your answers thoroughly before you decide you have finished and hand your answer sheet in.

I always do mock tests with my students before they sit their real exams and I have a set I have pinched from other tutors in the industry, however there are various websites that have mock tests where you can have a look and see for yourself how you get on. But over the years I have the same reoccurring areas of questioning that seem to always catch people out so I shall list here a few of them so you are aware of them and you can perhaps consider a bit of prior learning before you start your course. The most common one students always discuss after an exam is the fire classifications and what type of fire they are; class A is wood, paper and textiles, class B is flammable liquids etc.

You will more than likely be asked something on these classifications so be prepared, and I suggest you look at what type of fire extinguisher is required on each classification too. Another area student fall down on are the different colour coded Health & Safety signs in the workplace; red circle is prohibition, blue circle is mandatory etc. again always a good topic of discussion after an exam, along with the argument whereby some people seem to think a blue mandatory sign saying 'fire door keep shut' is actually a fire exit door. Not true, a fire exit sign is a green safe condition sign whereas a blue mandatory sign is telling you to keep the door shut to contain smoke and flames. Another area where students can fall down is the legislation Acts and their years such as The Private Security Industry Act 2001, Health & Safety at Work Act 1974 including the RIDDOR regulations of 2013, Human Rights Act 1998, Data Protection Act 1998, Criminal Law Act 1967, Licensing Act 2003 and The Equality Act 2010. I do not know if you will be asked questions actually on the Acts or their years, however it is always a good idea to at least take note during your course of what bits of legislation fall into which Act. Within the conflict management module the most common area that gets spoke about is what are a 'trigger' and an 'inhibitor'. A trigger is something which causes people to revert to violence whereas an inhibitor has the reverse effect, so think along the line that a gun has a trigger and a gun is bad therefore if you get asked the question of what is a trigger then think bad things and hopefully you will select the answer corresponding to what you believe to be something would trigger someone into violence.

Should you fail any exam you are given the chance to resit and this is normally free of charge for the first few attempts before the training company will start to be charged by the awarding body for the exam paper. I can only speak of the awarding bodies I have taught for but the majority do not charge you for resits and therefore the training company should not be charging you either. I agree fully with some tutors deciding that a student requires more training and for which there may be a charge made for the tutor's time, but to just sit a standard resit because you got a few questions wrong then there shouldn't really be the need to undergo any further training or be charged for the resit. Once you pass each individual module then you need never take that again and that stays with you. You will need to pass all individual modules to create your overall qualification of Door Supervision and to date you do not have to do any top up training except perhaps a Physical Intervention Upskilling day if you have not already achieved that.

Chapter Fifeteen

Upskilling

Physical Intervention has been a requirement for everyone undertaking the full door supervision course since June 2010 and is assessed by the tutor delivering the course. Some awarding bodies give you a multiple choice exam based around the theory whereas others do not, they get the tutor to assess you with a quiz style set of questions for you to complete on your own and in class. For existing door supervisors the introduction of them having to do physical intervention became mandatory in February 2013 meaning anyone wishing to renew their licence after this date needs to attend an Upskilling course before the SIA will issue the licence, however if anyone chooses not to undertake the Upskilling course then the SIA will down grade the door supervision licence to a security guarding licence.

The Upskilling does not just entail spending a few hours throwing each other about in a classroom as some people seem to think, the students actually have to top up their knowledge on the additional theory side of things that have come into the door supervision course since they would have originally passed their course such as an awareness of terrorist threats, considerations in dealing with 14 to 18 year olds and first aid awareness. The physical intervention side of it, the 'hands on' physical aspect of the training requires the students to undergo a predetermined set of physical procedures to meet the learning outcomes which I have previously listed earlier in the book. The style of physical training model they undertake is relative to the training company you opt to train with so some techniques will differ from other training models, however they all achieve the same outcome and that is to educate you and enable you to have a better understanding of physical intervention requirements for use within the security industry.

The upskilling should be completed over a period of one day with the guided learning hours being 12 of which 7½ must be contact hours; that is time spent in the classroom with the tutor. That gives a difference of 4½ hours which is normally achieved with what is called prior learning by way of course materials sent out to the students before they attend the course in order for them to learn and have some understanding before they attend the day's training.

Upskilling I find is one of the hardest parts of my job as a tutor. I have spent easier days on close protection jobs carrying out surveillance on my principal's threat or following the principal and their friends on a shopping trip around a packed City Centre all the time trying to maintain their safety along with maintaining my distance to enable them to have a normal existence. I find upskilling is hard because the students are all existing door supervisors, with some seemingly knowing more than me and who come in full of testosterone and want to show me or their partner, or both of us that they are the Patrick Swayze of their particular club and that they can do everything better. Truth is they probably can and they probably are a multi Dan black belt in every martial art going, been boxing since they were in nappies and now visit the local MMA club 7 nights a week, but none of that is worth a shit when it comes to the SIA's physical intervention day as they must meet the requirements of the learning outcomes without causing injury to themselves or their training partner. If anyone does not comply with the tutor's health and safety policy and messes around in a way that may cause an injury then the tutor can remove the student from the class without any questions being asked. When I teach the upskilling I put a lot of emphasis on the UK Law before I go into instructing the techniques that I am trained in, but I do make a point of informing the students before we start not to expect miracles and to expect to be leaving as a black belt in karate. The actual physical side of things is very low key which is something I do not agree with as I believe it should primarily be heavily geared towards self-defence for the door supervisor before any consideration is given to that of the attacker.

Having said that about existing door supervisors and it being a hard day to teach, I have had some fantastic students through on upskilling courses and have had some right laughs with students during the days training. I think the tutor themselves has to try and get the learning outcomes achieved in a serious way without anyone getting injured but at the same time bring some realism into the training and have a laugh with the students. A good days training will consist of scenario and role plays being introduced in a controlled way so the students can try and put into practice their newly learnt techniques in a pressurised environment whereby the tutor is trying to replicate what could happen in certain situations. But no classroom is ever going to replicate what happens in real life and the skills and techniques the students get taught can only really be put into practice when the real life situation occurs and the person they are trying to restrain is offering continued and aggressive resistance.

Chapter Sixteen

Applying info for SIA Licence

When you apply for your first licence spare a thought for me and every other person who had to suddenly gain their SIA licence when they first started to be introduced, as I had to wait near on 9 months for my first licence. Contacting the SIA was harder than getting a man in Space and when you did eventually get through the person on the end of the phone was either obviously very high in stress levels or not trained enough before being thrown into the action. Nowadays the application process is far simpler than years ago and the contact centre at the SIA has improved in leaps and bounds, except it is in Liverpool and you need a translator to understand them... that is a joke by the way before I get reported, I have lots of very good friends in Liverpool and the City is a fantastic place (except the football teams)! In order to apply for your licence you first need to register on the SIA's website as a user which is free of charge. You then proceed through the application process making sure you apply for a front line door supervision licence and indicate which awarding body issued your certificate. If you are unsure of this then make sure you ask your tutor or the training organisation where you did your course. I must admit at this point I have never done this procedure myself.

So how does the system work? First of all you need to take and pass the course, you cannot apply for a licence pending you passing the qualification because part of the checks the SIA carry out is to actually look that you have passed the course in the first place. The cost of the licence is £220 and it will be valid for three years unless you have it suspended or revoked, and this fee is non-refundable should they turn your application down. Now if you pay for the licence yourself then you are able to claim tax relief against your taxable income, and you will need to visit the HMRC website for more information on that. If you hold an SIA licence already then you only pay £110 for a second licence providing your existing licence is still valid and has at least four months left to run before it runs out.

You then have to pass a criminal record check, however if you have a criminal record it does not necessarily mean you will not get a licence because the SIA will make their decision based on if they consider your offences relevant to their decision, what the actual sentence given to you for the offence and how recent they were. On the SIA website they have a criminal record indicator which you can use to check whether or not you will pass their criminality criteria. Under the Rehabilitation of Offenders Act 1974 access to your criminal record is usually restricted however as it is in the public's interest for the SIA to have full disclosure of your criminal record in order to assess your suitability for a licence they are exempt from that restriction and will be allowed full access to your criminal record. If, at the time of your application, you have outstanding charges against you for any relevant offences then they will wait until the outcome of the charges has been reached before they make a decision. If the charges have not been resolved within a 12 month period then your application will be withdrawn and you do not received your application fee back.

There are a number of other checks they make on you when processing your application such as, your identity, your age (you must be 18 or over to hold a licence), whether you have completed the training, whether you have a criminal record and if so what is on it. They may also check any recent mental health problems where you have been detained or been subject to any other compulsory measures in the five years prior to when you apply for your licence. If you do have any mental health problems that are recent then you will be required to provide a current medical report outlining the condition and any ongoing treatments. Your right to work in the UK maybe checked during your application process also, however this has nothing to do with your employer's obligation to also check your right to work, and you possessing an SIA licence does not automatically mean your employer should take that as proof of your right to work. The SIA will not normally seek out information about you that could be held by other organisations such as the police or the local authority which has not been tested in a criminal court, but if this information is handed to them, or they have other information from their own sources (SIA warnings, Count Court judgements etc.) then they will consider it. In this situation the information will normally mean compelling evidence of criminal activity, anti-social behaviour, criminal association or activity that is likely to bring the industry into disrepute or indicates that you are not a fit and proper person to be issued with a licence. You do have the right to appeal any decision they make based on this fact.

You will need to provide documents that can prove your identity and your address. All the relevant documents you will be required to provide will be listed to you are the time of you completing your online application. All documents provided must be originals (not photocopies) and any that are printed not in English than you must provide them with both the original and the English translated copy (there is full guidance on the SIA's website regarding the translation of non-English documents. If you are sending the SIA your documents I suggest you send them recorded delivery, and once they have scanned and processed them they will be returned to you. Do not send any documents that you may need in the immediate future such as a passport just before you are due to leave the country. You will also need to provide a passport style photograph so make it a good one as this will be the image that gets printed onto your licence, and if you complete your application at a UK post office then the staff there will take the photograph for you.

The new system in place of online applications and post office completion of the application is a far cry from when I first applied for a licence and had to fill in a paper application form, send off my documents and passport photo and then wait ages for the return of my documents let alone the licence. Simply taking your documents to a post office after you have completed the online application, have the post office staff check your documents, take your photograph and take payment there and then really has made the application process a whole lot better. Once you have done all this you will be given an application number which is your online tracker of how your licence application is coming along. In most cases the SIA say to allow 4-6 weeks for an application to be processed, and this maybe the case for a new applicant however do not be surprised if it is processed quicker. Once you receive your licence you are able to then go off in the big wide world to ply your trade as a newly qualified and licensed door supervisor, but it does not stop there. You must keep the SIA informed of any address changes you make and submit to them your new proof of address, or any name changes such as you become married during the duration of your three year licence span.

Renewing your licence

The SIA will contact you roughly 4 months or so before your licence runs out and give you ample time to renew the licence. Remember you cannot work without a licence because you simply have 'forgot' to apply resulting in you allowing the current licence to expire which could end up with you being caught and fined. It cannot be any easier to renew your licence nowadays than simply ringing up the SIA and renewing over the phone in about a 10 minute phone call. In September 2014 I phoned up the SIA on a Monday afternoon to renew my Close Protection licence, I made the payment of £220 over the phone, confirmed a few security questions asked to me by the operator, listened to her relay be some legality wording and my new licence arrived in the post that Friday. So from the original days of the SIA where I and many other door supervisors waited weeks or months for a licence or a renewal, now it can be done all in a matter of days.

Chapter Fifteen

Looking for a job

Looking for a job on the Door used to be something very difficult, it was a very hard profession to get into until you had proved yourself and had experience. It was all about 'Not what you know but who you Know' Now don't get me wrong in this game its still about this to an extent but times have changed, they have changed a great deal.

Nowadays as it was back in the day if you had experience and had proved yourself and knew the right people it always was pretty easy to get fixed up with a Door job, but what if you didn't have the experience and without the experience you obviously hadn't had the chance to prove yourself then again its down to who you know and word of mouth, well that I would always say is the best way but times have changed very much in the world of working the doors.

There are many large companies now in the UK that basically act as agencies to supply Door Staff, some good and some bad but most of them operate on the same model and that is they employ a large number of door staff on zero hours contracts, that is the Door Supervisor is employed and has a contract of employment but has no fixed hours of work each week. Some weeks a person maybe required to work 30 plus hours and the next they may not be required to work any. Each week they will be given the shifts of various hours and in various venues.

This is a business model very similar to that used in various health care sectors and in particular Bank Nurses, this can be a good way to get a foot in the door as it were in working the doors but it's not for everyone. Many Door Supervisors work like this for a period of years and whilst this suits some it doesn't suit others. In my experience it seems that for people working in this manor end up getting a 'Permanent Door' when a Head Doorman at a venue that they have been sent to work in rates them and well, takes a shine to them for want of a better phrase, normally these are the best of the 'Floaters'.

Hourly rate is often griped about in this day and age and those new Door Supervisors don't get paid well, not well at all but then again what would you expect in any other role? Your new to it your almost in a 'Probationary Period' or training phase and really in this job you have got to earn your money and prove that your good at what you do, prove you have what it takes and that you are always there with your team.

Another good way of finding work on the Door is the internet with great forums such as 'Working the Doors' and 'UK Bouncers', Gumtree and believe it or not Facebook! There's always a job going for a good Bouncer on Facebook, which is if you know other people in the trade, I suppose it's the modern day version of word of mouth.

The best advice that I can give is talk to anyone you know who is either on the door or who used to be on the Door, there's a huge network out there of Doorstaff Old School and New and most of them all know each other even if they are out of the game, and be careful, be very careful who you work for.

Do all the checks you can on things like pay, when you will get paid, how you will get paid. Check for any deductions and check to make sure that your tax and NI will be paid.

Also check to make sure that you are covered by the necessary insurance that you need or you could fall foul of the law.

Also ask questions like 'Are you a subcontractor', this is very important to check or you may fall foul of what's known in the trade as the 'Subby Chain'. Basically what this means is that a company will take a contract on to supply Doorstaff, they then sub-contract that work to another company who may sub-contract to another company each one taking their cut. Often you need to wait for a long time to get paid if this is the case, basically the first company will not pay the second company until they get paid, and then the third won't pay until they are paid by the second and so on and so forth, and often the Subby Chain can break leaving you out of pocket.

Chapter Seventeen

How to deal with the after effects of violence for the first time

Violence "the intentional use of physical force or power, threatened or actual, against oneself, another person, or against a group or community, which either results in or has a high likelihood of resulting in injury, death, psychological harm, maldevelopment, or deprivation".

Lets look at the definition above before I talk about how to deal with the after effects. Violence in the Oxford Dictionary is a noun. A noun is a part of speech that is used to name a person, place, thing, quality, or action. We all know violent people but probably most of us chose to either not associate with them or not be around them when and if they turn violent. Violent places are everywhere, cities, towns and villages alike all have their violent areas, but again we probably chose to not frequent these violent places by choice. Violent things I can ascertain as being weapons and I am sure we all know weapons are a part of this modern world we live in, but again do we all carry them or use them? Hopefully not. Violent qualities is a talking point. We all possess violent qualities and I defy anyone to tell me they don't, but not everyone uses their violent qualities in certain situations they can or may find themselves in i.e. attacking someone or defending themselves. After all why do people attend boxing classes, or martial art classes, or self-defence classes? To me it is to assist them in becoming more confident should they get into any violent situations, so they can learn a skill that will ultimately save their life if god forbid that situation arose. I sent my youngest son to karate when he was 7 years old despite him wanting to be a footballer when he was older. What are the chances of him becoming a footballer? If someone told me when he was 7 that he would earn a professional contact with Southampton Football Club and I would proudly sit at St. Mary's Stadium and watch him run out for the team I have supported since I was 10 years old then I would of ploughed all my time, money and effort into pushing him towards that goal. However the reality is that would never happen. On the other hand could he get into a fight when he is a teenager and starts going out and about the pubs and clubs of Colchester? Yes of course he could and more than likely will do at some point. So my choice to put him through karate at the young age was my way of making sure if and when he encountered violence he would have some understanding and confidence in his own ability to deal with it. Since the age of 7 he has competed in and won many karate tournaments including British National Championships, International Championships and has fought all around the country including the O2 in London and as I write this book he is 2 gradings off his black belt. He has also boxed both conventionally and Muay Thai so I have peace of mind that he will at least be able to look after himself when he starts going out and about, but it is down to him if he chooses to use his violent qualities when the time occurs. This also applies to every single person reading this, or a person who goes out on the piss every weekend, or the business worker who works 9-5 in London and commutes every day. We all have violent qualities and some of us will use them to attack people, some will use them to defend themselves and some will have the qualities but chose to walk away as they do not like violence. But as human beings we are all animals and still have the animal instinct within us, the throwback to the caveman who had to hunt for food and fight to defend his territory. So again I defy anyone to tell me we do not have violent qualities, it's just some of us tone them and enhance them in preparation for when we have to use them. The last definition of the noun of violence is action. What is a violent action? By definition an assault is a violent action, and when you start working on the door this is the form of violence that you personally may face. In what form the assault reaches you I cannot define in this book, but it could range from verbal assault right up to a full on assault auctioning GBH upon you.

Now that has turned full circle and brought us back to the definition of violence *"the intentional use of physical force or power, threatened or actual, against oneself, another person, or against a group or community, which either results in or has a high likelihood of resulting in injury, death, psychological harm, maldevelopment, or deprivation"*. Let us not forget we live in a violent world either in far off countries where our British Armed Forces are fighting or in the pub around the corner. Violence is not limited to licensed premises though, I live in Colchester where this year there have been two separate violent and horrific murders where both victims were randomly stabbed to death, one at night and one in broad daylight, both on a public footpath and both with stab wounds one of which received over 100 wounds to his body. The whole town was on high alert when the second body was found with heightened Police presence in the town and parents wary of letting their children do the simplest of things like walk to school and walk up the shop. There was a fight in Aldi in the town resulting in someone being stabbed in broad daylight and in front of horrified shoppers, and this is just Colchester a town an hour outside of London, but it's a town where I know of people that it's rumoured walk around the town carrying guns. The bigger cities around the UK have a far bigger problem than what I have spoken about here however as we work on the door which is a licensed premises where alcohol is served, we will hopefully rarely see gun crime on the door, as the sort of violence we are going to face will 99.9% of the time be related around alcohol.

I recall my first violent encounter was when I was about 8 or 9 years old and I was playing in the local park with my Dad and sister or cousin. I have a very vague memory of a local thug throwing a knife at me and my Dad grabbing the thug and pushing him away. I can't remember what I had done – if anything at all – but I recall the image of my Dad grabbing the lad and throwing him to the floor. My Dad was never ever a violent person who to my knowledge did not ever get involved in violence, but spent over 22 years sailing around the world as an Officer in the Royal Navy and he told me it's a lie that a sailor has a woman in every port…. he has 2 or 3, so that would suggest my Dad was a lover not a fighter. My next form of violence that I remember was during secondary school when I started to get bullied from the older kids because of my name. I've had all sorts of jibes such as "do you watch Night Rider?" after the David Hasselhoff 80's TV show, "do you ride-her" making reference to when I started to have girlfriends and just general small minded idiots making fun of the name in general. Those who can be bothered to ask where it came from never ever question me again; I was named after my Grandad Arthur Ryder Lewis who was in turn named after an American Doctor Ryder who saved his life at birth. When I was bullied it started off name calling building up to the odd pushing, stealing dinner money and being spat at. When I was at school I never liked retaliating and would let the bullies win every time however one occasion I was walking my Mum and Dad's dog Raffles up the shop in Coggeshall where we lived. I remember turning the corner of the alleyway and sitting up the top was a few older lads, one of which would constantly take the piss out of me. My heart started pounding and my arse was dragging on the floor. I was about 13 or 14 years old and up to this point in my life had never boxed or been in any fight whatsoever, and

I remember wanting to turn round but I had been spotted. I also had to carry on as my Dad was cooking dinner and had ran out of something which is why he had sent me up the shop and the last thing I wanted to do was let my lovely Dad down, so I kept walking and when I got to the lads I kept my head down and walked through them. I heard the usual spitting sound so I knew somewhere down my back I had a big gob of spit dripping down, but then I heard my dog yelp. The main bully had kicked my dog as I passed, and there was no way I was going to let that go. I think because I had so much fear of these boys aged around 16 or 17 that my fear suddenly turned against them and I turned round and punched the closest one to me. I couldn't give a fuck if he kicked the dog or not but he was the closest one to me and I hit him right above his left eye. I only hit him once and it probably was not a very hard punch but it knocked him back off the wall he was sitting on. He stumbled and cowed down as I went to throw another punch which missed him, but it had the desired effect as all the other lads laughed at him. I stood there still angry and I have not got a clue what I said to them but I still can see the one I hit holding his eye and telling his mates to fuck off as he was walking away. From that day on I never got bullied again, and now you can see what I was on about earlier when I said everyone has violent qualities but not everyone uses them. Up till that point I had never thrown a punch in my life and the closest I had come to violence was watching Sylvester Stallone in Rambo, but when something had fired me up I used violence and saw the effect it had on the bullying as it stopped overnight. Afterwards I felt like I was floating on air, not because I had punched someone but because I had at last stood up for myself and felt proud that I now seemed to believe in myself a lot more. Eventually I would join a gym, build muscle and joined Chelmsford Boxing Club so bullying was a thing of the past in my life, but violence was just starting because one week after my 18th birthday I started my first shift on the door.

Now I am not going to list here all the violent situations I have been in, and I have previously discussed the most violent attack upon me in an earlier chapter. What I shall do is try and give you an insight into what I felt and how you may feel yourself as and when faced with violent situations. I can recall my first ever fight on the door as if it happened last night. I was working at The LA Club in Colchester which was a rough club but the violence was very well contained with a very good team of doormen, of course all older than myself as I was barely legal to go in there let alone work there. The club was a big ground floor venue with 2 rooms of music and could hold around 500 people at a push, and was situated in the far corner of a massive car park just outside the main town centre circuit. Just up the road was a small live rock band venue that attracted groups of Iron Maiden or Def Leppard leather jacketed motorcyclists who all had long hair and drank for England and who would carry on drinking in the club after the pub shut. We were also the last stop before the Colchester Garrison so would attract the soldiers who also drank for England or Scotland all wanting a drink before they staggered back into camp, so we often had fights between the two groups. One night there was a fight in the club and we got the group out into the car park, however as with most venues in a similar situation the fight carried on in the car park which was creating a problem as most of us doormen were outside and not dealing with the remaining customers in the club. Problem was we could not leave the groups to beat the fuck out of each other in the car park and we decided if we moved the group down the car park and out on to the main road then it was no longer our problem, so this we started to do. I was very young and lacking in confidence at this point, never really being allowed to get involved in too much violence as I was very well protected by the older doormen. However this turned into a free for all as the group of rockers fighting the squaddies was numbering around 25-30 in total and us 7 or 8 doormen were now all actively involved in herding this lot down towards the road. Suddenly I found myself isolated and trying to pull 2 athletically fit squaddies off a rocker who was taking a bit of a beating which I eventually managed to do, but as the squaddies left him alone he gained his composure and turned on me. Looking back I think he was that pissed and angry that he was being punched in the head while he was protecting himself that he didn't actually see who was hitting him, so when the squaddies left him alone he stood up and looked in the direction of where the punches were coming from and there I stood telling him to get out the car park. He then turned on me and started throwing punches at me which missed by a mile, but I instinctively called upon my boxing knowledge and smacked him right on the jaw to which he wobbled and on his way down he grabbed my suit jacket and ripped it as he hit the floor. Well I couldn't fucking believe this fat greasy biker had ripped my suit so while he was on the floor I kicked him full on in the face twice. He groaned and attempted to palm my kicks away but I carried on getting a few into his fat stomach and I then looked up to see most of the other group had got out the car park and were fighting on the street with the Police sirens getting louder and louder. I left this fat fucker laying in the car park and limped back towards the club as I had damaged my foot on his face.

I didn't really think too much about the fact that for the first time in a street fight I had knocked someone to the floor and then kicked them when down because I was now shitting myself that I was going to be arrested for fighting. It was only when I got home and was in bed that I started to go over what had happened and what I had done. I was actually horrified that I had kicked someone on the floor as deep down I am not a violent person and I hate to see that. Stand up and fight, win or lose it's a stand up fight as only cowards kick when their opponent is on the floor and I stand by that to this day. But for days and days after the incident I went over and over in my mind many 'what ifs' with thoughts ranging from "what if I he had hit me", "what would the other doormen say if I had got hit", "would they laugh at me", "what if I had got hurt". Let's be honest, if you asked anyone would they knowingly and willingly run into a group of blokes fighting they would probably say no, however when working on the door we are halfway across the club before we think anything like that and then that's the last thing on our mind so we ignore all the dangers that we could potentially face.

We only think about the 'what ifs' afterwards and then you play it over and over in your mind. With time and experience the thoughts will more than likely fade as it will be another situation dealt with and we move on. As Southampton's ex manager Nigel Adkins used to say "we draw a line under it and we move on", and at my stage in my career that is where I am at, and I imagine any long serving door supervisor will say the same. Unless we have a major violent situation we all draw that line under the event and move on, but when you are new to the game and you are faced with your first bit of violence it is all new to you and it will affect you. I remember thinking about kicking that bloke in the face for days and it really played on me and I did not like the image I could see being played over and over in my mind to the point it nearly made me give up the job altogether.

I have only ever done it the once since and then I was equally as angry with myself for doing it but in that situation I had a fight with an off duty doorman in Clacton and the fight went on for 3-4 minutes and again ended when I got a lucky punch in to floor him and something within me said 'kick the cunt while he is on the floor'. It is very unusual for a fight to last that long, and I can only put my actions down to relief and the thought I had that that man had to stay on the floor because if he had got up I was fucked. If you just so happen to be reading this and were the off duty doorman from London who had a fight at Rumours in Clacton on Valentines weekend 2001 with the head doorman then I apologise profusely for kicking you when you were on the floor, I will never apologise for my actions when I asked you to leave and you threw a punch at me, but for the kicking I will. Going back to the fight in the car park at The LA Club, a few years later I came across the biker I had kicked when I drove my dustcart onto the local rubbish tip to unload as he started working there. I spoke to him and let on what happened but he couldn't picture me although I too apologised for kicking him when down.

As I have said in my early years as a doorman whenever I was involved in a violent situation I would think about it for hours, days or sometimes weeks and go over it time and time again in my head to the point where it would affect me a bit. I would picture every second of the fight or violent situation and I would question if I had done the right thing, had I acted out of order, could I respond better verbally or did I let anyone down. Everyone deals with violence differently and if you take how I deal with it now as opposed to when I was younger, then I suspect people deal with it differently as they mature either in life or into the job. To me now violence comes and goes, and it doesn't affect me anywhere near as much as it used to when I was younger and less experienced. But when you encounter your first violent situation on the door how you deal with it will depend on what form the violence comes in, how old you are and how you react. The older you are then I feel you will deal with it better than the younger people reading this because the older we get the wiser we become and we learn to rationally take in things that happen to us and weigh up how or why it happened. By comparison when we are younger we fail to comprehend why someone has attacked us or we may take the verbal threats thrown at us too personally and become affected by them. The older I have become the more people I have become to know, and some of them are very violent people. I have friends in Liverpool who are very violent, I know people who know people in London who are very violent but when I was younger I did not know these people and was more or less on my own when it came to fighting my battles. The after effects of violence can also range from the bottom of the scale i.e. you have been a witness to a violent situation to the top of the scale i.e. where you have been the victim and are seriously injured. But who I am to say that you being a witness to a violent situation is actually the bottom of the scale? We are all individuals and what I see as low scale violence another may see different and vice versa. Few years ago I was running The Silk Road in Colchester and we had a massive fight on Christmas Eve resulting in me being badly bashed up on my face. I spent virtually the whole of Christmas day in agony and barely able to see out my swollen eye, but I thought nothing of it. By comparison when all the beheading videos started becoming an unwelcome scene on the internet I searched and watched one out of curiosity and I had to turn it off after a few minutes. The sight I witnessed and the sounds I heard were horrendous and it affected me for weeks even though I did not see it at first hand.

The way I deal with violence is to first of all look at myself and work out was I the intended target for the violence; if I wasn't then I forget about it almost immediately but if I was then obviously I have upset someone at some point and I need to address why and in what way I have upset that person. I make sure that I offer people respect and I treat people how I would wish to be treated myself. On the doors I have met and befriended people who I would never want to upset, local gypsies, known hard men, successful boxers etc. but at the same time I earn their respect by treating them as a normal person and if they play up they have to leave. Treating people with respect means if or when they kick off with me, or offer violence towards me then it has been their choice and I didn't have anything to do with my actions other than doing my job. With this reasoning for violence towards you, and assuming that you have not been the cause of it I would make it the norm that you quickly forget all about it and move on otherwise it will eat away at you and will result in you giving up the job or losing your bottle when situations arise again and therefore risk not only your own safety but that of your colleagues. If the violence towards you has been brought on because you have intervened in a fight and ejected both parties then again you should start to have the mind-set that you were not the intended target of the violence but more so it was the upshot of you doing your job. In these situations though there is the chance that a single individual or group may take extreme offence to you having removed them from the venue and take it out on you. This I think is the most common cause of violence you will face and is always the one that if you retaliate you could end up either hurt or face being arrested and prosecuted resulting in you losing your SIA license. Remember we all have a right under UK Common Law to self-defence however your defensive action must be reasonable in the circumstances[3], what the law does not allow for is revenge and retribution. What can happen in these situations is that the aggrieved individual or group could come back to attack you at any time and you should never let your guard down, never think as they have left that they are never coming back. In Clacton many years ago 2 blokes were ejected from the club for being far too drunk and very aggressive towards other customers who were out to have a good time. These 2 blokes took a major dislike to the fact that they were asked to leave and spent a fair while laying down threat after threat including they were coming back to shoot

---

[3] For more detailed explanation on the Law concerning reasonable force I suggest 'Understanding Reasonable Force' by Mark Dawes.

us all. These 2 could not hardly stand up let alone hold, aim and fire a weapon so we all dismissed their pathetic claims that we would all be dead. About an hour later the police arrived and asked if we had had some trouble with a few lads involving shotguns, to which we half-heartedly laughed at their threats when we removed them from the club. Now what with me being a very good judge of body language and people's reactions, the policeman who I was talking to was a good laugh, always messing about and cracking jokes however on this occasion he just stood stony faced as our half laughs faded away. Even before he spoke another word by arse hit the floor, my stomach over took my bollocks on route also to the floor as my bollocks shot up into my mouth as I braced myself for what I suspected was news that the 2 blokes had been arrested on route with shotguns. I was nearly right except the circumstances around the police and the blokes meeting was far worse. They were so pissed that whilst driving back towards the club they crashed their car on a bend and at speed, with the car stopping almost immediately as it hit a concrete and metal fence around a small green on a crossroads. One of the blokes had shot through the window of the car and was found up a tree and to this day is paralysed, and the other was killed. Shocking for the families of the 2 blokes, both had their lives ruined by drink driving, but imagine how many other lives could have been ruined if they had made it back to the club. When the police arrived on the scene 2 loaded shotguns were found in the boot of the car, and just by chance they had crashed right outside the house of a doorgirl who worked for the same security firm and who had been outside the club when the blokes got ejected. She informed the police of the bloke's intentions that they were heading back to the club to shoot dead the doormen hence why the police attended and told us of the news concerning the crash. I cannot begin to imagine how to deal with gun crime violence but that was the closest I have ever come to it, and the chances were if they had succeeded in reaching the club I may never have even had the chance to deal with it.

Dealing with violence is a unique thing that you will develop as you go through your career and build up experience. I worked for many years as a wheel clamper and during my time I faced many an upset motorist where I had to take £150 off them to release their vehicle or it would have been towed away. I got threatened a few times, asked the age old question of "how do you sleep at night?" to which many times I was itching to reply back with "Horlicks mate" but I never did as taking £150 was bad enough let alone wind them up even more. But surprisingly enough I have faced far more violence and verbal abuse while working as a doorman than I ever did as a wheel clamper. People will turn on you when you work as a doorman and they will not think twice about attacking you if they are that way natured and/or pissed enough, but normally they return the following night or weekend to apologise and request that it is all forgotten and you let them in. How you approach this is a measure of how you deal with violence and dealing with it for the first time will be a struggle. Do you except the apology from someone who has spent half the night calling you a fat cunt, or saying they have fucked your mother or sister, or they are going to stab you or they know where you live. In Clacton one night I threw two brothers out and they stood there giving me the usual bollocks saying they knew where I lived to which I just ignored and humoured them a bit, trying to defuse the situation. However after a few minutes one of them recited my address to me and that put a whole new perspective on it. My girlfriend at the time who I lived with was the deputy manager of the club and was working with me that night with our 3 children at home and the 16 year old babysitter. Suddenly the threat was real and I called my girlfriend down and spoke with her saying I had to get home in case they turned up. I phoned Michael the boss of the security company I worked for and told him I had to get home quick explaining why but he told me to stay where I was and he would sort it. Within half an hour 8 doormen and Michael were sitting in my house just in case these two boys returned with their very large family from London, but of course they never did. But for days after I was wary when I left the house as they really did know where I lived, and they could have been watching me or my family as we left the house. They were from a large London family that had settled in Clacton and were not a threat individually but together with all their family members would have been a problem for me on my own. What you need to do in situations where you get threatened is try and ignore the plastic threats and worry about the real ones if and when they return or happen otherwise you will start to lose interest in the job and probably end up leaving. Try and have come backs to humour the verbal threats with such as when they say they have fucked your Mum ask them was she good. Don't show them you are effected by what they say when you know they have not fucked your Mum. If they say they will come back and get you just ignore it because the majority who say they will come back never do, but never ever let your guard down because there is the small minority that will come back. Try not to antagonise the people when they say they will come back, don't tell them to try and knock you out now rather than coming back – despite how tempting it is – as this is not a professional approach especially as the SIA's code of behaviour doesn't say we must act that way. What you can try to do is just except this is the behaviour we are going to face in our line of work and hit it head on despite the fact that we have a right not to be abused at work. I used to get abuse when I drove a dustcart for a living because I was holding up the traffic for 5 minutes along a road and someone wanted to get past, yet when it came to summer time and the very same person stuck behind me giving me abuse wanted all their grass clippings taken away then I was the best thing since sliced bread. That proves that violence is situational and not always predetermined or purposely directed at you as an individual, however you need to understand that and as I have said do not let it get to you.

There will be those amongst you that will say violence will not affect you and you will go and pass your course, get your licence and go find yourself a job. You may have the odd fight, minor abuse or even a small amount of violence and you may think you handled and dealt with it ok, until you have a really violence situation and you may then reconsider your approach to dealing with it. It may not be your thing, something you thought you could handle but as it turns out you can't. I have worked with some fantastic doormen who I then recruited to work with me as wheel clampers and as soon as they face a group of blokes snarling at them to take the clamp off their arse goes, the remove the clamp for no charge and never do the job again but they can work as a doorman in a team and fight as hard along with the best of them. Violence has a very wide spectrum to discuss because as I have said what some people find really violent others don't and vice versa. Some people will head off to the Middle East to work as a close protection operative in hostile environment but I wouldn't, and it has nothing to do with me having no interest whatsoever in guns, but why would I want to go and work in an environment where I could be shot at but on the other hand I will go to work on the door – sometimes a one man door – where I could at any time be stabbed.

How I dealt with my violent attack from Michael in 1996 was that I knew I had not upset David with the intent of him trying to head-butt me but I was simply doing my job and unfortunately for me I was on the receiving end of the violent retribution from the whole family and half the doormen from another club. But what did affect me was the after abuse which was being directed towards my then girlfriend and the stomach churning I got whenever anyone mentioned David's name to me. I would never ever want to go through that attack on me again but something deep within me kept telling me I had to do something about David and his continued movements of frequenting my girlfriend's restaurant where she worked a waitress. Unbeknown to me David had been going in and really upsetting my girlfriend for months, but she chose not to say anything to me in the hope that he would go away, which of course he never did. One night I was sat at home and her sister came round to see Tyler who at the time was a baby and she asked my girlfriend in front of me if David was still upsetting her. Of course I knew nothing of this and I then got out of the pair of them all that had been going on resulting in me having the stomach churning feeling again which I did not want. I had now had enough and decided enough was enough and I had to confront David once and for all, so I got up, went to my car and drove around town for ages looking for David in the hope that I would see him. I was never going to find him if I was honest but in my mind I was doing something to combat this feeling I was having and not liking, it was my way of dealing with this particular violent event that had occurred a few years before hand. I was fucked off with the nerve of a man who had attacked me, been badly hurt by me with the result of me being hospitalised in a revenge attack and now harassing my girlfriend to the point that she was at home crying and not wanting to go to work. What right did he have? To this day I can honestly say if I had seen David that night I would of probably attacked him and more than likely of been arrested for the first time ever carrying out a premeditated attack, however after driving around town for hours I suddenly saw Michael standing on the door of a venue. At this time I was working in Chelmsford and was not working for Michael at all so it was at a time of our uneasy peace, bit like our own mini Cold War. I stopped my car, got out and walked up to Michael to which we shook hands pleasantly before I gave Michael a few choice words concerning his brother and his pathetic actions towards a girl because he obviously could not get to me. I was well aware it was not Michael's fault and I never was rude or threatened him, but I made it very clear what I would do to David if I was to see him and that I would face the aftermath from Michael and his mob again if need be. In that situation, a few years after the initial violent attack on me, this is how I was now dealing with the violence. I was actually telling the man who had hit me so hard that I had pissed myself that I was going to attack his brother again and face the consequences if David did not leave my girlfriend alone, and guess what... it stopped. I have never asked Michael if he spoke to David, I have never asked Michael if he even told anyone that I was looking for David that night, but suddenly the abuse towards my girlfriend stopped and she could go to work and do her job without being petrified David would come in. I want to reiterate that David and I are now friends and we have spoken many times about his pursuance of my now ex-girlfriend/wife where he still apologises to this day.

How will you deal with your first violent encounter no one knows, I certainly don't as I don't know you. But what I do know is that the only person who can judge that fact when it happens is you yourself, but you will have a battle with your inner self before you come out the other side either confidently by brushing it aside or by deciding that being on the door is not for you. Do not be ashamed if you think fuck that I can't deal with this violence, just do not carry on with the job if you cannot deal with the violence that you will face. Cut your losses and get out of the industry not because I want all door supervisors to be able to 'have a row' but because I do not want anyone getting hurt due to you not being able to handle the violence and you freeze. Be honest with people about how you feel as and when you face violence for the first time, but most of all be honest with yourself and do what you feel is right for you and for everyone around you. I also work as a close protection operative and have worked on jobs where there is a high threat, where there is a strong possibility of a kidnap attempt on my Principal but I chose to still do the job because I know I am capable of dealing with the threat and possible violence the team or I will encounter, however I will not go out to work in the Middle East oil fields where I need to carry a weapon in order to protect the Principals. What is the point because I know I will freeze the second I hear a real gun firing in anger at me and that will put the life of everyone at risk so I don't do it.

Remember violence does not come looking for you personally, we are in an industry where violence is part and parcel of it and we put ourselves at the forefront of the job to tackle it. That is why we have a front-line licence from the SIA because we are on front line duties and our main aims while working as a door supervisor are to make sure everyone has an enjoyable experience in a safe environment, even if that means us having to deal with the violence in order to achieve that aim. People do not go out on a particular evening with the intention of offering violence towards you, but situations may prevail over a course of events that put you and violence on course for a collision. I was born in Portsmouth but since the age of 9 have supported Southampton which is the cause of raised eyebrows when I chat to people. I don't hate anyone in life but it is bred into us Southampton fans to hate the Portsmouth fans and vice versa, but truth be known I don't hate the fans, I don't hate the football club as my Dad used to go and watch Portsmouth a lot when he was based in the town during his Naval career, however when it is match day I have a little giggle if Portsmouth lose. When Portsmouth played at St. Mary's a few years ago they equalised in injury time with one hell of a goal after we had took the lead minutes earlier I could of punched anyone with anger when the final whistle went and it did not have to be a Portsmouth fan. That would have been a violent act towards someone because of a situation that had angered me, not because I hated that person and 9 times out of 10 that is how the violence will find you on the door.

Before I end this chapter, and as I have touched on the Southampton and Portsmouth rivalry, I just want to say WTFILN! Any Saints fans reading this I bet you are smiling and now singing the song, any Pompey fans than you are probably regretting buying the book, but honestly from the heart I hope Pompey recover and we can have the South Coast Derby again.

Chapter Eighteen - Complete

Do's and Don'ts

DO - Get Licensed. Getting licensed not only shows that you are legally allowed to undertake duties as a Door Supervisor, but also it gives you the BASIC training needed to begin to do your job well. If an establishment is willing to hire you without a license you might want to reconsider as both the Employer and The Employee (You) are breaking the law and face possible fine and / or imprisonment.

Do - Show up on time – Even better, show up for your shift a little early. It comes back to taking your job seriously. By showing up early, you can find out what is going to happen during your upcoming shift, prep any gear that you haven't dealt with already, do a walkthrough of the establishment, and check in with the venue manager or Head Doorman

DO - Dress appropriately and look the part and It is your responsibility to be ready when the shift starts. That means having your earpiece, radio, SIA License etc. on ready to go.

DO - Ask questions – If you don't know the answer to a question, ask someone else. If you don't know how to do something, ask. If you want to learn something, ask.

DO - Be patient – No one is perfect. Not your boss, not your co-workers, not the intoxicated patrons, and certainly not you. When things go wrong or when there is yet another problem to deal with, take a deep breath and approach it patiently and calmly. Going into any situation – especially when dealing with an intoxicated individual – with a hot head will get you NOWHERE. Being patient allows you to listen better, be more objective, and hopefully solve any conflicts with a clear head.

DO - Keep training – Learn new skills, constantly. Whether it is how to check IDs, learning more about intoxication, studying martial arts, or practicing conflict resolution, any new skills that you acquire will help you become more proficient at your job, which in turn helps you become a PROFESSIONAL.

DO - Be a mentor…or look for one – Once you've learned some skills, start teaching others. Teaching someone is the best test of whether or not you really understand a concept. You need to have complete understanding of any concept in order to teach. You can't just 'kind of get it' or know it just well enough to get by; you MUST know your subject.

DO – Treat everyone equally and never discriminate on any grounds

DO - Back up Team. Always always always back up your team no matter why, you never know you may be relying on them for you life one day!

DON'T – Drink on shift of be under the influence of alcohol when on duty

DON'T – Take Drugs on Duty or be under the Influence of them while on duty

DON'T – Weapons

DON'T - Don't get into fights – It seems ridiculous to have to say it but your job is to prevent fights, not start them. I am not saying that you shouldn't defend yourself, but if you are starting the problems…find another job.

DON'T – Fall foul of the opposite sex. There always someone hanging around of the opposite sex, don't be blinded with them and don't take anyone home it will always come back to bite you. I am sure you have all heard of the phrase 'Door Whore'

DON'T – Take bribes to let people into a venue, not just money but payment in kind will be offered to you on a regular basis

DON'T – Make it personal, it's just a job

DON'T – Think you're the 'Big I am' just because your on the door, because sure as eggs are eggs it will get knocked out of you.